IPSWICH PUBS

SUSAN GARDINER

AMBERLEY

First published 2016

Amberley Publishing
The Hill, Stroud
Gloucestershire, GL5 4EP

www.amberley-books.com

Copyright © Susan Gardiner, 2016
Maps contain Ornance Survey data.
Crown Copyright and database right, 2016

The right of Susan Gardiner to be identified as the Author of this work has been asserted in accordance with the Copyrights, Designs and Patents Act 1988.

ISBN 978 1 4456 4499 8 (print)
ISBN 978 1 4456 4519 3 (ebook)

All rights reserved. No part of this book may be reprinted or reproduced or utilised in any form or by any electronic, mechanical or other means, now known or hereafter invented, including photocopying and recording, or in any information storage or retrieval system, without the permission in writing from the Publishers.

British Library Cataloguing in Publication Data.
A catalogue record for this book is available from the British Library.

Typesetting by Amberley Publishing.
Printed in the UK.

Appointed GPSR EU Representative: Easy Access System Europe Oü, 16879218
Address: Mustamäe tee 50, 10621, Tallinn, Estonia
Contact Details: gpsr.requests@easproject.com, +358 40 500 3575

Contents

Map	4
Introduction	5
Brewers & Breweries	6
Ipswich Pubs	12
Bibliography	95

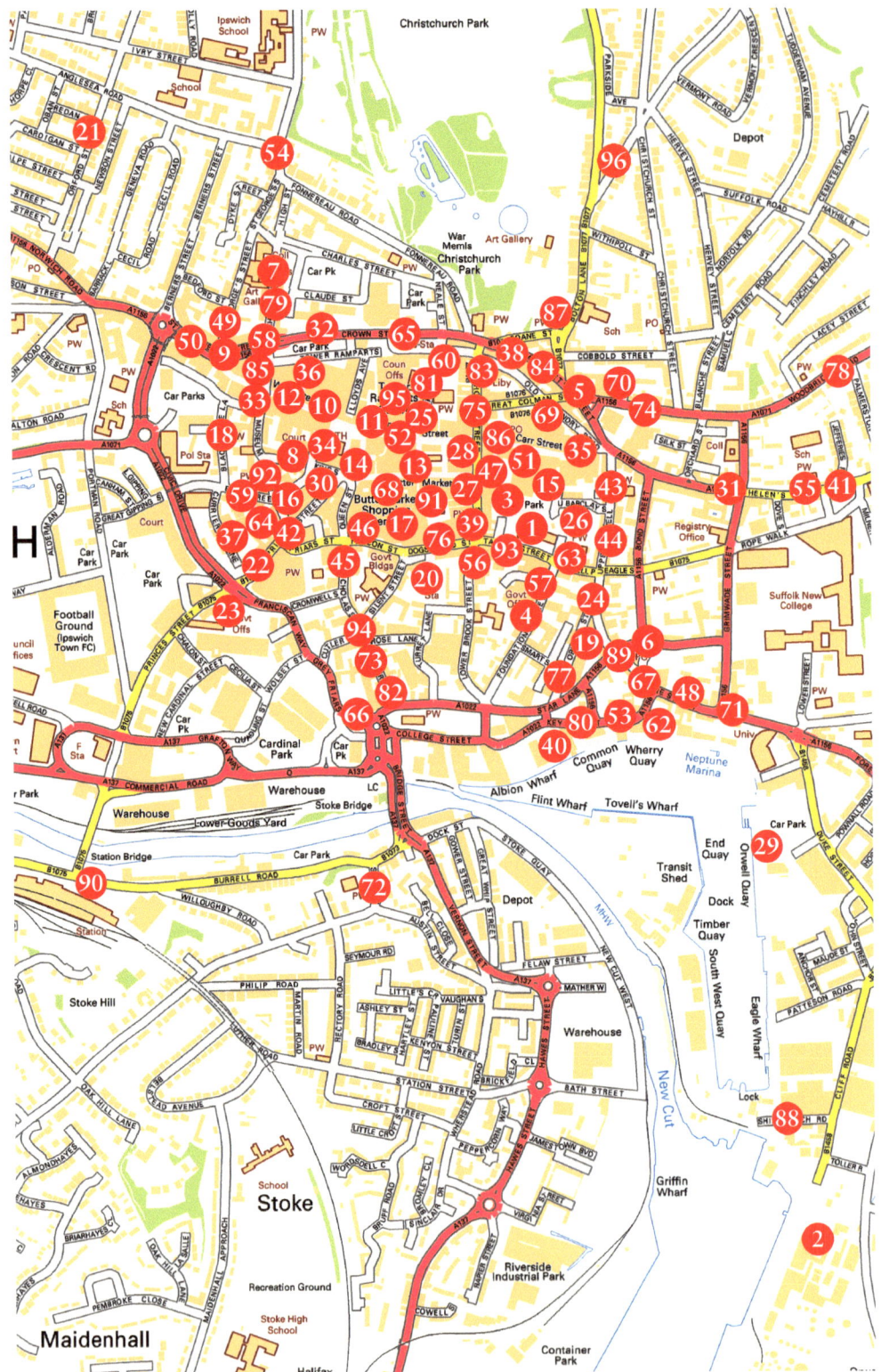

Introduction

Ipswich, known for hundreds of years as a 'town of taverns', had so many inns, hotels, taverns and public houses, that it is impossible to do each one of them justice. I have therefore concentrated on town centre pubs, with the addition of a few important taverns in the port area and on the outskirts. Having by necessity been selective, I've chosen what I consider to be the most interesting pubs, although that is somewhat unfair to the many small beerhouses and street corner pubs that I've omitted. I use all the terms for drinking establishments interchangeably, to avoid monotony, although they are by no means synonymous. A beerhouse, for example, could only sell beer and not wine and spirits. Inns and hotels had overnight accommodation for their customers. The dates of tenancies and ownership of some of the inns described in this book are estimated, based on trade directory and census records, and are not necessarily the exact dates that landlords came and went. In some cases, it has been possible to find more exact information in reports of magistrates' 'Brewster Session', when licenses were awarded and, frequently, withdrawn.

For those interested in more detail, the Suffolk part of the CAMRA website and the books of David Kindred are recommended. Frank Grace's superb history of St Clement's, the poorest Ipswich parish, *Rags and Bones*, also provides a picaresque account of its many beerhouses and pubs.

I would like to thank the following people for their help: Kingsley Fletcher for photography, proofreading and help with research, Dan Lightfoot, Ken Lightfoot, Richard Mainwaring, Alasdair Ross, Steve Lewis, Gavin Barber, Suffolk Record Office, Suffolk Libraries, and the British Newspaper Archive.

Brewers & Breweries

Just as Ipswich was a town of taverns, it is equally true that Suffolk was a county of breweries. The happy accident of being an area noted for the quality of its barley, with access to pure water and good transport connections to bring hops in quickly from Kent, meant that Suffolk was the perfect place to set up breweries and the county has long had a reputation for producing the best quality ales. Today, brewers like Greene King in Bury St Edmunds and Adnams in Southwold are internationally successful, but for hundreds of years brewing was a domestic affair, often performed by women. Female beer-makers were known as brewsters or ale-wives in the Middle Ages and documented East Anglian examples include 'Clarice le breweres' in Colchester and Margery de Brundall.

The Suffolk entry in the Domesday Book of 1086 does not mention any brewers or breweries in Ipswich itself. According to local historian, Vincent Redstone, 'beer brewing was the occupation of a few families residing in St Clements.' In 1483, there were five 'alien' or foreign brewers living in the town, suggesting that there may have been quite a number of small breweries, as there were few immigrants at that time. A number of people were recorded in the Ipswich tax assessment records as brewers. These included Jose Bakker, Gerard Dyrykson and Henry Foslowe, all from Zeeland; Cornelles and Peter Berebrewer (Netherlands); Gerard de Deventor, from Utrecht; Simon Petirson, 'servant to Gylys Johnson, beerbrewer' from Cologne; and Gylys Johnson, a 'brewer and merchant' from Liège in Belgium.

If incomers did not make up the majority of brewers in Ipswich, the large number of them suggests that there was, at least, a flourishing industry from the middle of the fifteenth century. In his short history of inns and taverns in Ipswich, the Revd Evelyn White told us that

> Brewers of beer had to be specially licensed, and were forbidden either to sell beer at an under price, or to brew any beer for sale in other than the ancient brewhouses, by continuance of ten years at the least.

London beer was forbidden to be introduced into the town, or sold by retailers.

Ipswich local government regulations, constituted after King John granted the town its royal charter in 1200, laid down some rules for brewers and gannokers (ale-wives):

> And all that comen Brewers and Gannokers shall selle a galon of the best ale for ijd [two pence] And not above And a galon of the Seconde ale for id (i.e. one penny) and not above upon peyn of grevous amercyment And that all comen Brewers and Gannokers shall sell by just and true mesures.

It seems the brewing of beer in Ipswich was closely regulated from the beginning, long before anyone thought of controlling its consumption.

The Ipswich accounts between 1559 and 1602 still exist and they mention three brewers: Merrell & Fuller, Smithe (both 1568) and Carsye in 1571–72. These small breweries were often, if not always, connected with an alehouse or tavern, usually on the same premises, a practice that continued through to the nineteenth century and which has been revived by the craft brewery movement of the present day. Some of them were the precursors of much larger breweries that went on to become major industries, the most well-known being Tolly Cobbold. By the nineteenth century, as many as twenty-five breweries could be found in Ipswich trade directories, although the majority of these seem to have been small, short-lived operations. There were a few, however, which became more substantial and were established enough as businesses to become major local employers and in the nineteenth and twentieth centuries there was a series of almost bewildering mergers and takeovers resulting in the establishment of the four larger breweries in Ipswich that would come to dominate the town. These were:

1. Brook Street Brewery, Upper Brook Street

Starting in 1856, this brewery was originally owned by Cullingham & Blogg, a merger of Charles Cullingham with Ashton Blogg, who had previously had a small brewery in Foundation Street. It was probably where the Unicorn Brewery was later. From 1873, its proprietors were Charles Cullingham and Frances Blogg, but by 1885 Cullingham had become the sole proprietor. Also known as the Steam Brewery, it was a large concern, owning sixty-nine public houses and inns, as well as maltings. When Charles Cullingham retired in 1888, the company was acquired by Tollemache.

2. Cliff Brewery, Cobbold & Co.

Thomas Cobbold, a member of a family of Suffolk farmers and maltsters, started a brewery in Harwich in 1723. The decision to move to Ipswich in 1746 was made because the water at the Essex site was unsuitable for the production of the highest quality beer and the Cobbold family already had the Holywells estate, near the River Orwell in Ipswich, where springs of pure water could be found. Cobbold experimented with transporting the Holywells water to Harwich by boat, but it became obvious that there were other advantages to moving to Ipswich, where the Cobbolds had interests in banking. The first brewery that was built at The Cliff, or Cliff Quay, consisted of wooden buildings, and the complex of buildings that we know as the Cliff Brewery was built as late as 1894–96 and designed by William Bradford, who also designed the Unicorn Brewery in Foundation Street. The Cliff Brewery was extended further in 1904.

When the Unicorn Brewery closed in 1923, the houses belonging to its owners, Catchpole & Co., were shared between two companies, Cobbold & Co. and Tollemache, bringing the number of pubs owned by the Cobbold family to 270. The Cobbolds were dominant in the town for many years, maintaining their interests in other aspects of Ipswich public life including banking, politics and football. It was not until 1957 that an amicable merger with Tollemache's resulted in the well-known Tolly Cobbold brand, which would be successful until the 1970s, a period in which big breweries began an aggressive policy to take over smaller concerns around Britain.

Despite the Cobbolds having historically conducted their business in a benignly paternalistic manner, the 1970s saw some industrial conflict. In 1977, brewery workers went on strike over pay negotiations. The strike spread to Cambridge, Colchester and Norwich. It had an immediate effect on the supply of beer to public houses in Ipswich and elsewhere and also led to the story of Tolly Cobbold's famously louche director, John Cobbold, being stopped from entering the Cliff Brewery by a picket line. The pickets let him through with the (possibly cleaned-up) comment 'You can go in, Mr John. You do bugger all anyway.'

Barely a week after the strike had been settled, Tolly Cobbold was taken over by the Ellerman Shipping Group. The firm's relationship with the town of Ipswich further declined following government intervention in the brewing industry in 1978, which forced it to exchange six public houses in Ipswich for seven in Essex. Following a relatively short period with the Ellerman Group, which was taken over by the Barclay brothers current owners of the *Daily Telegraph* leading to an even greater depletion of the company's various properties, Tolly Cobbold was acquired by the Brent Walker leisure group. Brent Walker sold off even more public houses to Grand Metropolitan and eventually in 1989 it was announced that brewing would be moved from Ipswich to the Lion Brewery in Hartlepool. Sixty-six Ipswich brewery workers lost their jobs.

Despite a management buyout in 1990, beer production at Cliff Quay stopped forever in 2002. Since then, the historic buildings have become so derelict that it was named as one of the most at risk Victorian buildings in the country. Recently plans to convert the site to housing and arts facilities have been broadly welcomed by the residents of Ipswich.

3. Ipswich Brewery, Upper Brook Street

Tollemache took over the Brook Street Brewery from Charles Cullingham in 1888 and it became known as the Ipswich Brewery Ltd in 1896. The year before Tollemache took over, the brewery had produced over 9,000 barrels of beer and the acquisition of Cullingham's brewery and pubs shows the scale of the ambition of this aristocratic family turned brewers. This was a state-of-the-art steam brewery, which stood where the Tacket Street car park is now. They continued to expand, purchasing the houses belonging to Catchpole & Co. in 1918 and the Essex Brewery in 1920. They also

The Brewery Tap, with the old Cliff Brewery behind, is in Cliff Cottage, originally owned by the Cobbold family.

The dominating presence of the old Cliff Brewery with Cliff Cottage, now the Brewery Tap, below.

This old Tollemache mirror is now at the Brewery Tap.

bought out several other small East Anglian breweries until, in 1957, the firm merged with Cobbold & Co. to become the famous Tollemache & Cobbold or Tolly Cobbold Co. It soon moved from Brook Street to an expanded Cliff Brewery.

4. Unicorn Brewery, Foundation Street

Beer production had taken place on or near the site at least as early as 1839 when Robert Paul was listed in a trade directory as a brewer there. In 1842, it was sold by Robert Garrod at an auction in the Great White Horse Hotel and was clearly a well-established and well-equipped concern, judging from this advertisement in the *Ipswich Journal*:

> The capital newly erected and compact brewery, situated in Foundation St, with the excellent and well arranged plant capable of brewing eight to 10,000 barrels annually; with a comfortable residence and an inn known by the sign of the Unicorn, attached, and the undermentioned well-accustomed public houses and licensed beer houses.

Although Ashton Blogg was listed a brewer in Foundation Street in 1855, Nathaniel Catchpole appears to have taken over the Unicorn Brewery soon afterwards. The company changed its name from Catchpole & Co. to the Unicorn Brewery Co. Ltd in 1918 but it is thought that brewing only continued there until 1923. The firm owned fifty-six public houses, all taken over by Tollemache's Brewery and Cobbold & Co. It had been a worthwhile enterprise. When Nathaniel Catchpole died, at his home in Whitton, in 1909, he left an estate of £263,628.

Brewing was moved to the Cliff Brewery in the early 1920s and a member of the Catchpole family, the former owners, started a mineral water bottling plant there, Talbot & Co. Ltd, producing lemonade, ginger beer and cider. According to family member, Richard Catchpole, they were awarded the franchise for selling Pepsi Cola during the Second World War, a lucrative contract given the number of USAAF personnel based in Suffolk at that time. Soon afterwards, the factory was bought by Cottrill & Cantrill of Colchester and closed down. The building has now been converted into residential apartments.

The Unicorn Brewery, second only to its Cobbold rivals.

Ipswich Pubs

5. Admiral's Head, St Margaret's Street

The Admiral's Head was a fine building. Its exposed timbers and ornate chimneys suggest it might have been constructed in Tudor times, or even earlier. It dated from at least 1740, when it was recorded in a window tax account.

It was named after Admiral Vernon, who died in Nacton in 1757. Vernon was nicknamed Old Grog after introducing slices of lime to navy rum rations, to combat scurvy, a disease caused by vitamin C deficiency. He was MP for Ipswich, so it was probably local pride that meant this pub kept its name long after, according to Revd White, 'the sign painters were everywhere employed in touching up Admiral Vernon into the King of Prussia.'

A starting point for carriers on their way to Woodbridge and East Suffolk, George Garrett was the landlord in 1810, succeeded by Richard Caston, who was there until he retired in the mid-1850s.

The Admiral's Head was popular with supporters of the Whig MP, Rigby Wason, who was elected for Ipswich in 1841 but was quickly unseated after he was found guilty of bribery. The pub also catered for spectators at public executions. In 1845, Maria Sheming was the first woman to be publicly hanged in Ipswich for thirty years, after she was found guilty of poisoning her illegitimate infant grandson. The local press reported that a drunken and rowdy crowd had gathered to witness it, so large that it spread 'from the gaol to the Admiral's Head' where no doubt they kept themselves suitably refreshed.

In October 1898, the owners, Tollemache, agreed to surrender the license of the Admiral's Head in exchange for a full license for the Shoulder of Mutton in Upper Orwell Street and the premises became Turner's antique shop.

6. Angel, Angel Lane

The Angel was mentioned in a document of 1528 when the borough charged rent for its sign. It was 'THE Inn of the neighbourhood' according to Revd White. Leonard Thompson, in *Old Inns of Suffolk*, wrote that it was the:

principal of the neighbourhood in pre-Reformation days and reputed to have been a house of rendezvous for Cistercian monks. It shared with the King's Head, the White Horse and the Cross, the distinction of the halting place for refreshment on the occasions of the perambulation processions, notably those of the parishioners of Saint Clement's at Rogationtide.

The Angel had a less salubrious aspect however. Letting single rooms in the yard to young women led to a reputation for prostitution. According to Frank Grace,

> the landlord was described as running a 'loose' house and allowing his female lodgers to entertain men. Maria Cook, for instance, had a tenement in the inn yard. Late one night a group of men broke into the pub, stole drink, and wandered down to the dockside where they joined a mate on one of the ships before returning to the inn yard for a drinking session in her room. On another occasion … around midnight in May 1880, an elderly man was reported to the police by neighbours when he knocked on doors in Angel Lane, and stumbled into Mrs Stannard's yard at No. 5. He was arrested for being in enclosed premises for an unlawful purpose: he had apparently called out to Mrs Stannard 'My name is George, let me in.' In court, the policeman who had apprehended him stated that the prisoner was the worse for drink and had said to him that he did not know where he was, but thought he was in Angel Yard and was after 'a dark woman… Her name is Easton' who like Cook was a prostitute. The man, George Finch, cut a rather pathetic figure in court. He was wearing three medals and was stated to be an army pension and ex-policeman who had been discharged for health reasons.

The Angel became run-down in the late nineteenth century and was almost derelict before it was finally demolished to make way for Fore Street public baths in 1906.

7. Arboretum, High Street

Originally at No. 29 High Street, but later at No. 43, the Arboretum was named after the arboretum that was designed in 1851 as a place of quiet recreation in nearby Christchurch Park. An advertisement was printed in the *Ipswich Journal* in July 1852:

> TO BREWERS & OTHERS.
> TO BE SOLD BY PRIVATE CONTRACT, WITH IMMEDIATE POSSESSION,
> A valuable BUSINESS PREMISES, known as the ARBORETUM HOTEL, in St Matthew's Parish, Ipswich, containing spacious cellarage, entrance hall, two well fitted-up parlours, tap room, scullery well supplied with water, and other requisites; a Concert or Club Room, 33 feet by 16 feet 6 inches; airy bath-rooms, stable, cart lodge, and large yard, with good entrance from main street.

Between 1855 and 1858, the landlord of the Arboretum was William Lankester but by 1870 it was in the hands of Ebenezer Tooke. Tragedy struck in June of that year, when his sister-in-law, Lydia, the twenty-eight-year-old wife of his brother Alfred, drowned herself and her nine-week-old baby, also called Lydia, in the River Gipping. She was clearly suffering from what would now be recognised as post-natal depression. Ebenezer was called to give evidence at the inquest. He gave evidence that Lydia and the baby had left his premises shortly before the tragedy took place. The Tooke family remained as landlords until the early twentieth century when it was run for many years by Arthur Hogger. The Arboretum did not get its full license until 1956, when the landlord was Leslie Ward, and presumably until then had only been able to sell beer.

After a short closure in 2008, the Arboretum reopened and for a few years operated as a popular gastropub. In 2013, it was taken over by the former landlord of the Grinning Rat in St Helen's Street.

8. Arcade Street Tavern, Arcade Street

Standing at the junction of King Street and Elm Street, this bar is in a very old part of Ipswich. Some existing buildings nearby date back to the fifteenth century, and it was probably near here that Ipswich's castle stood before it was razed to the ground in about 1173. Arcade Street itself is relatively modern, having been created in the mid-nineteenth century, as an extension of King Street through to Museum Street. Before that, the site was occupied by a bank belonging to the Ipswich & Suffolk Banking Co. The manager, William Ingelow, lived above the bank with his family, including his daughter, Jean Ingelow (1820–1897), who would become a popular writer in the late Victorian period. The bank failed, however, and in 1850, the Ipswich Lighting & Paving Committee decided that a short stretch of road would be cut through, making the arcade that gave the new street its name.

No. 1 Arcade Street has had several incarnations in the form of various wine bars and restaurants. It is currently a successful bar selling craft beers.

The Arboretum on the High Street, named after the Ipswich arboretum in Christchurch Park.

The nineteenth-century arcade cut through from King Street to Museum Street gave this popular venue its name.

9. Assumption, site unknown

An inn called the Assumption certainly existed in Ipswich in medieval times. It is mentioned in official records in 1527 when the landlord was charged sixpence a year to be allowed to keep a sign outside. Although the site of this tavern has never been found, it may have been associated with the shrine of Our Lady of Grace in Lady Lane, now a rather depressing alleyway where Westgate Street meets Norwich Road. In the Middle Ages, this was a place that was visited by thousands of pilgrims, a shrine devoted to the Virgin Mary and the site of a chapel where a royal wedding took place. There were several inns in this area, presumably making a good living from providing accommodation to the pilgrims and their servants. Many of these taverns had names that related to the story of the birth of Christ, such as the Three Kings, the Salutation and the Angel. The Assumption of the Virgin Mary, when she was supposedly taken up to heaven, was a very important day in the Catholic calendar and particularly among Marian cults. It is quite likely that an inn of this name was situated somewhere close to her shrine. Some historians have suggested that the inn might have been in Lady Lane itself.

10. Bantam Cock, Westgate Street

The Bantam Cock appears to have been somewhere close to the Crown & Anchor in Westgate Street, although there is a little confusion about its actual location. There was also a beerhouse called the Bantam Cock in Carr Street, according to the reports of the Ipswich Police Courts. Such reports frequently featured many of the Bantam Cocks' customers. For example:

> *Riotous Conduct.* - Frederick Warne, Potter Street, St Helen's, was charged with being guilty of riotous conduct and refusing to quit the Bantam Cock, Westgate Street, on the night of Saturday last, between 10 and 11 o'clock, when requested to do so by the landlord, Mr Balls.

There were countless reports of this kind in the Ipswich press and Emma Archer, who kept the Bantam Cock, along with her husband James, in the 1870s and 1880s, appeared in court several times. In July 1881, she gave evidence against a labourer, William Metchem, saying that she saw him with his hand literally in the till on 26 May of that year, while she was having tea there with her young niece. Metchem, who had a previous conviction for a similar offence was sentenced to six months' hard labour.

By the 1890s, the name had changed to the Ivy Leaf. George Martin was recorded as a beerhouse keeper there in the 1891 census; his widow, Elizabeth, originally from Clerkenwell in London, was there in 1891. Albert Plume, followed by William Overett, succeeded them as beer retailers until 1922. The Ivy Leaf closed in 1933.

The name of Bantam Cock suggests that there may have been a connection with cockfighting, which was certainly a popular pastime in Ipswich, but it seems unlikely that it took place here. It's unlikely that there was a yard of sufficient size to accommodate cockfighting, such as the one at the nearby Cock & Pye in Upper Brook Street, where the sport certainly took place.

11. Barley Mow, Westgate Street

The Barley Mow is the name of a well-known English drinking song. Popular in the pubs of Suffolk, it was sung regularly at places like the Blaxhall Ship. It's a cumulative song or round, which may have been associated with harvest celebrations, each round proposing a drink to every aspect of the pub from the smallest drinking vessel to the landlord himself. The trick was to remember the correct order of quart pot, pint pot, half a pint, gill pot, quarter gill, nipperkin, brown bowl, half gallon, gallon, half barrel, barrel, landlord, landlady, landlord's daughter, slavey, drayer and company (those drinking in the pub) despite having drunk a toast to each. Given the song's popularity in Suffolk, it's not surprising to find it as a pub name in Ipswich and, at No. 36 Westgate Street, it was in the heart of the town, an area heavily populated by public houses and beerhouses. It stood on the corner of Westgate Street and the bottom of what was then known as Barley Mow Lane.

The Barley Mow was open as early as 1823 when it was run by Henry Fowell. In 1830, the landlord was Thomas Hooper. It was sold by auction, along with a brewery, three shops, a house and stables on 18 April 1861. The auctioneer's listing gives a good description of what the pub was like at that time:

> The BARLEY MOW, a noted and old-established TAVERN and SPIRIT SHOP; presenting a handsome plate-glass front to Westgate Street at the corner of Barley-Mow Lane, in St Matthew, with corner, front and side entrances, appropriated to the several departments of the business; capital Cellarage, Smoking and Porter Rooms, Counting Room; family sitting and sleeping-rooms, with a substantially-erected Brew House; and all the spacious Cask and Bottle Stores, Yard and Premises, adapted for carrying on the extensive and lucrative trade which has been for many years and attached to the Property.

Soon afterwards, the borough magistrates allowed the renewal of the Barley Mow's license – the applicant's name was given as Larner. The license had previously been suspended 'till proper urinals were made'. The whole Barley Mow site was put up for sale again in October 1862. This time the advertisement gave an impression of how substantial the brewing capacity on the site was:

> ... a very substantial brick building, about 40ft. by 37 ft., recently erected and adapted for receiving a Plant for a Family ALE BREWERY; with paved floor, a strong brick arch to support a copper, cooling floors, with louvres, &c., and having in the basement capital Ale and Porter Store, in which is a Well, affording an ample supply of the finest spring water. A paved passage leading from the brew-house to Barley Mow Lane.

The whole property was bought at auction by the brewers, Catchpole & Co., for £1,800. The reason for the sudden sale was obvious from this rather optimistic notice to debtors that was published at that time:

> J. J. Mills later of the Barley Mow, Ipswich, requests all those indebted to him to pay their debts to his father, James Mills, Stonemason, Back street, St Clement's, Ipswich, forthwith, as he is about leaving England.

In 1864, an excavation took place at the Barley Mow and 'a jar filled with English coins was found as the depth of several feet'. According to the report, the jar was removed by the owner of the premises and nothing else was known about the coins. In 1966, the Suffolk Institute of Archaeology reported that 'medieval and Saxon pottery, including Thetford and St Neots ware, from the site of the Barley Mow' had been found and given to the Ipswich Museum.

In November 1866, the *Ipswich Journal* announced that Barley Mow Lane was to change its name, a decision which it applauded:

> 'Barley Mow Lane' is not a dignified name for a street in the centre of a large town, and ... now that the lane has been improved into a street, to couple it with High Street, whose name in future it will share. We trust that Barley Mow Lane will see the propriety of increased circumspection of conduct and manners upon its alliance with the respectable neighbour as High Street.

12. Bear & Crown, Westgate Street

In the nineteenth century, the Bear was Ipswich's main Whig pub, as well as being a renowned coaching inn, but it was a well-established and respectable inn long before that and was in existence at least as early as 1696, when according to the town accounts, it received payment for billeting soldiers. In 1739, Abraham Knapp, a carrier, was advertising that his cart stopped at the Bear & Crown to 'take in Goods and Passengers' on its journey from Stowmarket to London.

The Bear was one of Ipswich's favourite places for cockfighting, and this advertisement in the *Ipswich Journal* is typical:

> On Tuesday and Wednesday being the Twenty-sixth and Twenty-seventh of December 1751, will be a MAIN of COCKS fought at the New Cock-Pit at the Bear and Crown in

Ipswich; the Gentleman of Essex against the Gentleman of Suffolk and Norfolk; to shew thirty-one on each side, for Five Guineas a Battle and Twenty the odd.

The notice was signed by Edmund Orford, who was landlord at that time.

The Bear was offered to be let or sold in October 1743, and again put up for sale in May 1746: 'To be Sold, and enter'd upon immediately, The BEAR and CROWN in Ipswich, an old-accustom'd INN, all Freehold, with good Stabling, a Brewhouse and Garden.'

In April 1787, the Bear was again for sale: 'a Capital Inn, now in full trade, ... in the occupation of the owner who wishes to retire from business.' Despite changing hands so frequently, there is no suggestion that this was a place that caused its owners or tenants to ruin themselves, financially or otherwise.

In 1791, the (unnamed) landlady of the Bear was a victim of T. H. Moreland, who was being held at Newgate Prison on a charge of bigamy:

Moreland came to this place from Chelmsford in April last with an assortment of pictures; soon after which he married his second wife, who kept the Bear and Crown, one of the principal inns in this town. He did not however remain long in this situation, which he considered as too servile, but disposed of the house; and with the assistance of her property *flashed away*, bought a whiskey, and went to London.

In 1828, the Bear was the centre of huge public interest when an inquest was held there on the death of Elizabeth Squirrel, the housekeeper of William Rodwell, an Ipswich solicitor. She had been stabbed to death by Rodwell's butler, Thomas Churchyard. The jury brought in a verdict of manslaughter, a large crowd awaiting its decision in the inn's yard. It was a bizarre case, in which the victim left a note claiming that if she was killed by Churchyard, he had been provoked and she forgave him. Churchyard was acquitted at Bury Assizes in April 1829.

At the end of March 1829, C. Spall sold all the household effects of the Bear & Crown by auction. He moved to the Lion at Eye. At the same time, Thomas Lappage was advertising the Suffolk Commercial Hotel (later the Bear & Crown) to the 'Nobility, and Private and Commercial Gentlemen.'

The Bear & Crown became part of the Suffolk Hotel in 1828–29. Some sources say that this followed a fire, but if so, it was not serious enough to be mentioned in the local press. An 1835 advertisement gives a good description of the hotel's facilities:

To be sold by auction, by the instructions of the Executors of the late Thomas Lappage, deceased. ... The house is spacious, and the rooms 40 in number, comprise of 8 parlours of good dimensions, three of which are divided by shifting partitions, beautifully fitted, making when removed a splendid ballroom, 54 ft long by 20 ft wide, and 13 ft high; 25 sleeping rooms, nursery, bar, liquor bar, large kitchen, back house, larder, coal house, store rooms; the whole extremely arranged and replete with every convenience; extensive wine and spirit cellars, a tap, well accustomed; stables, capital, (often accommodating 100 horses) with lofts and corn chambers over.

The hotel was bought by James Rowell and the Suffolk Hotel became known as the yellow house, the unofficial headquarters of the Liberal party in the town. When Samuel Read drew James Rowell in his sketchbook of prominent Ipswichians, he drew a back view of him standing in top hat and long coat, legs planted firmly on the floor, holding up a glass as if making a toast. He was clearly a dominant and formidable figure in Ipswich life.

By 1871, the hotel, managed by Ellen Buckle, was known as the Public Hall Pub, after the new Public Hall nearby (where Primark currently stands), but reverted to the name of Suffolk Hotel by 1874. In 1891, it had become the Suffolk Stores and no one was living on the premises, it finally closed in 1905. Eventually the Oriental Restaurant, or Café, opened on the site.

13. Bee Hive, Buttermarket

There were several pubs called the Bee Hive in Ipswich, but perhaps the most well-known was a mock-Tudor pub which opened in 1899 at Major's Corner. It closed and was demolished in 1960, and had been run by Charles Quinton (1899–1906), Leonard Leaney, Ernest Barrington Thorp (1930s) and Tom Beckerleg. In the 1950s, Beckerleg's sister, Mrs Grace Tremayne, moved to Ipswich from Cornwall after separating from her husband and she became the landlady for many years. Her daughter and son-in-law, Mr and Mrs Eric Gordon Hughes took over until the Beehive's closure, when they moved to the Live and Let Live in Wherstead Road.

Before that, there had been an earlier Bee Hive, at Nos 18–20 Buttermarket. This public house became the Grand Hotel during the 1890s. A separate drinking establishment continued next door as the Bee Hive Tap. Judging by mid-nineteenth-century court reports the alleyway by the Tap was used for prostitution.

A Bee Hive existed in Ipswich in 1814, as it is mentioned in a newspaper advertisement for the creditors of one Richard Cross, a baker. No address was given then, but 'that old-established Tavern, the Bee Hive, situate in the Old Butter-market' was available for rent in January 1824. In 1830, White's trade directory listed the Bee Hive Tavern, at No. 16 Old Butter market. The landlord was James Goodhew. In February 1833, the stables and hay lofts at the back of the inn suddenly collapsed, almost killing Joseph Miller who was standing nearby at the time.

According to historian John Blatchly, Thomas Crisp and his wife Mary Ann kept the Bee Hive in the 1840s.

> The rent, due to the Tower churchwardens as owners, was £5 a quarter. Here on one Wednesday each month the Perfect Friendship Lodge would meet. By 1844, Crisp appears to have abandoned the trade of publican for that of clothes broker.

The Bee Hive had its own Assembly Rooms and it appears to have attracted several local societies. Meetings of the Saxonian Masonic Lodge were held there and the Memnonians, an all-male musical society, also met there. Despite being officially dedicated to music, the Memnonians appear to have been a political group, leaning towards Conservatism. Things were not always harmonious among the Memnonians.

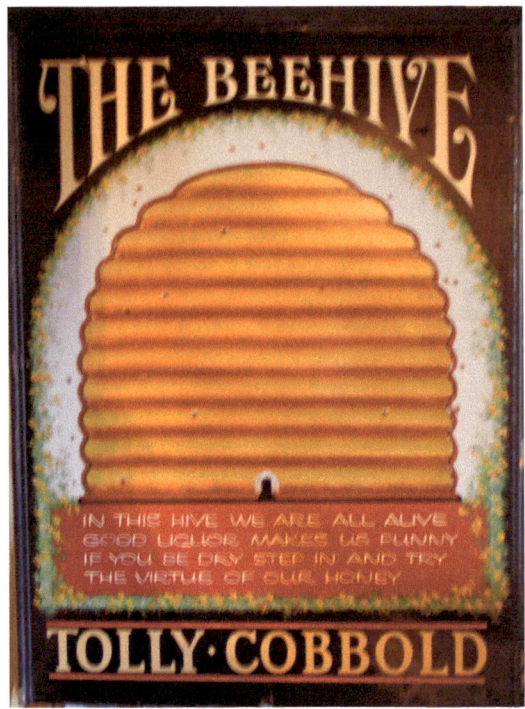

The sign of the Bee Hive (courtesy of the Brewery Tap).

In 1847, Samuel Mullett, former landlord of the Bell on the Cornhill, brought a case of assault against Mr W. Williams, after he tried to attend a meeting at the Bee Hive. It appears that there was a scuffle after several members attempted to throw Mullett out. They had moved to the Bee Hive because of problems with some members whom they were clearly trying to exclude from the new Memnonians. The implication was that they had moved in an effort to exclude members such as Samuel Mullett. His allegations could not be substantiated and after he admitted that 'he did not recollect the language he used because he was so frightened,' the case was dismissed.

By the time, the inn became the Grand Hotel, the old building had been replaced by one with a castellated front which contained an elegant Palm Court where a resident orchestra played. It is now a listed building from which the Cheltenham & Gloucester Building Society operates.

14. Bell, Cornhill

The Bell stood on the corner of Westgate Street and the Cornhill at the end of the row of buildings which included the Golden Lion and Mannings, all three among the oldest pubs in Ipswich. The building that replaced it, on what was known as Bell Corner, is a familiar one, having been for many years after the pub's closure the premises of J. H. Grimwade & Son, tailors.

It was known as the Blue Bell from the mid-eighteenth century and its location by the market place meant that it was often used as a meeting place for traders. In 1838, the Bluebell was sold by auction, as the property of the Manor of Waylands. It had been repaired recently at considerable expense and included wine, beer, spirits and coal cellars, two parlours, a large porter room, a spacious bar, kitchen and back kitchen, a large dining room, four bedrooms and two attics.

For some years it was known as the American Stores and sold wines and spirits and it has been used as a retail outlet for a succession of enterprises.

15. Belvedere, Cox Lane

The name Belvedere comes from the Italian for 'beautiful view' (*bel vedere*). It seems inappropriate for this rather ordinary public house in Cox Lane, which backed onto the Tollemache brewery. The original building was demolished in the late 1930s and replaced by a slightly grander one. It was briefly known as the New Belvedere, but a new landlord, Ernest Webb, is thought to have brought the name of his old pub, the General Gordon in Upper Barclay Street, with him. The pub seems to have been in the hands of the Webb family until at least 1952, when a Kelly's Directory lists the landlady as Mrs L. L. Webb. At some point the pub's name was changed again, this time to Earl Roberts, another important military figure who died of pneumonia during the First World War. Towards the end of its days, the Earl Roberts was a well-known music venue in Ipswich. It closed in 1999 and the building has since been demolished.

16. Black Bell, Museum Street

The Black Bell was on the corner of Museum Street and Elm Street. The name is unusual, but may have been simply a way of distinguishing it from the Bell on Cornhill and the Old Bell at Stoke. It was an inn from at least 1754 until 1936 when it was

This Victorian building replaced the Bell, or Blue Bell, and was later the premises of Grimwade's tailor shop.

knocked down. When it was put up for sale by auction in February 1769, it was described as

> a Freehold Messuage, call'd the Black Bell, in St Mary Elms Parish, Ipswich, now in the occupation of Israel Sallows; consisting of Parlour and Kitchen, in Front; a Back Kitchen, Brewhouse & Cellar, five Chambers, two Garrets, two stables, and a good Piece of Garden-Ground.

In November 1852, the landlord, William Hackney, was in court following a complaint against him by Col Bence of the local militia, for refusing to accommodate soldiers who were billeted there. It was alleged that Hackney had refused a private, William Jackaman, use of a frying pan and poured hot water onto the soldiers' beds so that they were too damp to sleep in. In return, Hackney alleged that Jackaman had brought a very young girl into the pub insisting on taking her to his room. Counterclaims were brought, mainly that Hackney was extremely drunk and ran a very bad house. A police officer, Superintendent Mason, told the court that the soldiers were so uncomfortable there that they would rather sleep at the police station. Hackney was not convicted, but only because Col Bence had requested that he should not be. He was ordered to pay the considerable expenses of an alternative set of billets for the militia. Col Bence remarked that he wanted to thank Superintendent Mason 'for the great forbearance which they (the police) showed in keeping off the populace upon the occasion of the regiment attending church.'

In October 1868, the household furniture and trade utensils of the Black Bell were sold at auction, because the landlord, John Webb, was leaving the business after several years. The 1883 Ipswich Brewster Sessions, renewed the license of landlord, George Kerridge, but only after cautioning him: 'the Mayor informed the landlord … that the police reports respecting his house were very unsatisfactory.' Mr Kerridge replied that he had attracted some disruptive people by the music that was played there, and had occasion to send for the police. Mr Grimwade (from the bench) advised him 'when you get people in do not give them any drink,' which seems to be odd advice for a publican.

The Black Bell closed in 1936, its last landlord being Sidney Godfrey, previously of the Duke of Kent.

17. Black Boy, St Mary-le-Tower

The Black Boy was one of only twenty-four inns recorded in the town's tax assessment of 1689. It was in the parish of St Mary-le-Tower. David Kindred thinks that the Black Boy was in Tower Street or Tower Lane, and quotes a 1684 record referring to: 'a payment of four pence petty rent on behalf of ye Black Boy.'

It may have been called the Black Boy and Still at one time, which was a very unusual name. The name of The Black Boy is quite common in England and, although it is thought by some to refer to slavery – the black pageboy being a fashionable accessory for the wealthy in the eighteenth century – the name was also used to commemorate the restoration of Charles II, whose nickname it was. This explanation seems possible given the local, unsubstantiated story that the fugitive Prince Charles hid in a secret room in the ancient house in the nearby Buttermarket.

18. Black Horse, Black Horse Lane

The Black Horse is a beautiful old building, dating back to the fourteenth century, but its current popularity stems from more contemporary interests. It is where many Ipswich Town football fans gather before matches at Portman Road, which is close by, and for some years it has been a venue for heavy rock music. It must have been a private dwelling for a long time before it was an inn. It was not one in 1689, when records show that there were only two licensed houses in St Matthew's parish – the White Lion (now the Golden Lion) and the Crown, the site of which is unknown.

According to Leonard Thompson, in *Old Inns of Suffolk*, 'the most outstanding architectural feature of the Inn is its Tudor doorway, with its oak-panelled and studded door of pure Jacobean workmanship.' It has retained many original features to this day.

In 1758, the Black Horse was described as 'an antient and very good-accustom'd Publick House.' In the eighteenth and nineteenth centuries, it was known to be a place where recruitment for the army took place. There are two examples of army recruitment taking place here with literary connections. Margaret Catchpole's brother, Charles, enlisted in the 33rd Regiment of Foot here, under the false name of Joseph Dedham, according to Richard Cobbold's *History of Margaret Catchpole*. Another Black Horse recruit was William Candler, husband of the Suffolk poet, Ann Candler, who joined the militia here in 1777, leaving his wife and six children behind in Sproughton. Ann would eventually spend twenty years in Tattingstone workhouse.

In 1809, the Black Horse was put up for sale, this time described as having 'a large and well-planted Garden; and with or without eight acres of Arable and Pasture Land.' It was let again in 1820, the occupier leaving 'for another situation,' the advertisement described the pub as having a good trade. It was owned by St Peter's brewery at this

The Black Horse, close to St Mary Elms church.

time. One landlord, Robert Clarke, who died in 1830–31, was an insolvent debtor and a prisoner in King's Bench Prison in London. In 1830, the landlord was Christopher Goss, who was also a dealer in hay and straw. Later in the 1830s, the tenants were Jacob Mills and his wife. He was fined 5s for Sabbath breaking, when he allowed people to drink there during Divine Service.

Leonard Thompson's description of this pub, suggests that it was rather more upmarket in the late nineteenth and early twentieth centuries than it is now:

> At one time the Black Horse was renowned for the excellence of its Old ale, the consistently splendid condition of which was said to be due to the perfectly balanced temperature of the cellar. During the latter part of last century the inn is reputed to have been a fashionable mid-morning rendezvous for doctors, lawyers, and the tradesmen the St Matthew's. Today [1946] the Black Horse still fulfils all the essential offices of the English inn; members of the theatrical profession especially have good cause to remember the quality of its hospitality.

19. Blue Anchor, Lower Orwell Street

Sometimes described as a beerhouse, the Blue Anchor – also known as the Anchor – was certainly an inn for some part of its existence, as it is recorded as having boarders, mainly local labourers and, occasionally, itinerant musicians.

Its landlady between 1881 and the mid-1890s was Adelaide Andrews who several times appeared in court for selling alcohol at prohibited times, mostly on Sundays. She appears to have been let off on each occasion by claiming that all those drinking there were *bona fide* lodgers, even though newspaper reports often claimed the excuses given were greeted by laughter in court. The Anchor appears to have been one of the town's rougher pubs. Andrews herself had tried to have a customer prosecuted when she refused to leave after being found 'fighting on the floor.' Regardless of this, the license was renewed in 1893. Owned by Catchpole & Co., the Blue Anchor closed in March 1915.

20. Blue Coat Boy, Old Cattle Market

The Blue Coat Boy stood on the Old Cattle Market, close to where the bus station is now. The building supposedly dates back to 1620. It is not a name that is unique to Ipswich but it refers to something purely Ipswichian – a charity school that was founded in the town in 1709. The school educated children if they were sponsored for £1 a year, and their parents were members of the Church of England.

The Blue Coat Boy was open in September 1774. It was owned by Thomas Cole in the late eighteenth century. He died in Duke Street in 1803 having moved to the Turnpike, Rushmere Heath. In 1830, the landlord was William Scotford and it was listed in trade directories at No. 38 Silent Street. The landlord in the 1840s was John Wells, who appears to have had a certain notoriety in the town. In March 1847 he appeared in court charged with committing assault with a poker on George Andrews, a shopkeeper from Somersham. It seems that there were a number of similar incidents and, in this case, Wells' maidservant at the pub told the court 'as soon as I heard the row I went to get the fire-irons out of the way, for in a row master always flies to

Since closing as a public house, the Blue Coat Boy has been a series of restaurants.

them.' Wells' defence was that Andrews had threatened him with violence over a raffle, but he was found guilty and sentenced to pay a fine of £10, with a further £60 costs, and to be imprisoned until he paid the fine.

The pub was advertised in February 1855: 'Public house to let. Known as the Blue Coat Boy, situated in the Cattle Market, Ipswich, doing an excellent trade. Valuation moderate. Apply to Mr J Artiss, at the above Inn.'

During the Second World War, when so many USAAF servicemen were based in Suffolk, the Blue Coat Boy was designated as a place where black soldiers and airmen could drink. Such racial discrimination came at the request of the American authorities. During the war, the military police in Ipswich arrested two white servicemen after they 'displayed a pugnacious attitude towards all colored soldiers, especially those seen in the company of white girls.' The Blue Coat Boy closed in 1986.

21. Brewer's Arms, Orford Street

The Brewer's was a beerhouse in the 1840s and so could only sell ale. In March 1878, the Borough Quarter Sessions heard the case against William Gosling, described as a pensioner, who was alleged to have stolen £8 and a great deal of furniture, bed linen and clothing belonging to the then landlord, William Ledsham. He had left the premises, along with Mrs Ledsham, while her husband was working at his other job, in the Foundry. He came home to find the place stripped bare. They were discovered, pretending to be a married couple at a Bradford pub and brought back to Ipswich for trial. Gosling was found guilty and sentenced to two months' hard labour, because it was ruled that Mrs Ledsham had no right to any of the property and he was therefore guilty of larceny: 'though a woman might take away the goods and chattels of her husband without committing a larceny, yet if she were accompanied by a man for the purpose of adultery, then the man was guilty of larceny.'

Tucked away, north of Crown Street, the Brewer's Arms continues to be a thriving town centre pub.

The sign of the Brewer's Arms showing the crest of the brewers' guild.

In September 1870, the landlady, Iona Gardiner, received a warning from magistrates that her license might not be renewed 'on account of warnings by the police and various irregularities.'

The Brewer's Arms finally received a full license in 1962. Still thriving today as a small, back-street pub, it is owned by Greene King.

22. British Lion, Princes Street

Standing on the corner of Princes Street and Edgar Street, the British Lion was a typical working man's pub of its time, with a Union flag for a sign. A stone lion stood proudly on the roof. In 1850, the landlord, Robert White, brought charges against James Wade, a customer, at the Borough Sessions, accusing him of stealing 'five fowls'. The police found portions of five birds at the defendant's home, 'cut up ready to be made into a pie.' Wade was acquitted because 'no conclusive evidence had been given to identity,' although it's not clear if this is a reference to the identity of the thief or the chickens.

The British Lion was described at various times as a beerhouse, an inn and a hotel. For many years, from about 1880 until 1895, it was run by Longland Maxwell, followed by his daughter, Drusilla.

On the route from the town centre to the railway station, the British Lion was popular for discos and other events until its closure and demolition in 1972. It was part of the site that would be redeveloped and on which the award-winning Willis building, designed by architect Norman Foster was built.

23. Cardinal's Head, Wolsey Street

One of many pubs to be named after Thomas Wolsey, this was one of many beerhouses in the town centre for much of the nineteenth century. In 1849, the landlord gave evidence at an inquest held into the death by drowning of a thirty-two-year-old blacksmith, James Raynham White, who had been drinking heavily there on the night he died. The pot-boy also gave evidence at the inquest, saying that the deceased was the last person to leave that night. It appears that White fell into the Gipping on an unfenced stretch of the river and accidentally drowned.

James and Mary Fulcher kept the inn in 1851. Ten years later, James' widow was running it alone. By 1881, it had changed its name to the Zulu Tavern, and the landlady was another widow, Mary Atthowe. It is likely that the name was changed to celebrate the British victory in the Anglo-Zulu war of 1879. Later publicans were Robert Smith, landlord from about 1888 until after 1901, followed by his widow, Ellen Smith. The last tenant was Mrs E. Wright. She ran the Zulu for more than fifty years until her retirement in 1965, when she was presented with a retirement gift by Lord Tollemache, whose company, Tolly Cobbold, owned the pub.

24. Castle, Lower Orwell Street

The Castle was one of Ipswich's oldest inns, and was one of only twenty-four mentioned in the town assessment of 1689. Its name presumably refers to Ipswich Castle, which was razed to the ground in the twelfth century. Despite its age, very little is known about its early history, even its exact location in Lower Orwell Street.

The landlord between 1830 and the mid-1840s was John Roper, who was also a carpenter. From 1850 it was run by William and Kitty Ward, but by 1855, the tenant was Samuel Cracknell. By 1859, it was in the disreputable hands of Austin Catley from Hull. He was later landlord of the Falcon and was probably the same Catley who was reprimanded by local magistrates for allowing immorality in the gardens of the Freemasons. At the Castle, he got into trouble for knowingly harbouring prostitutes. In 1868, he had moved to Coggeshall in Essex where he got into serious debt and by 1871, he had returned to his native Yorkshire.

In the 1870s the Castle was run by George and Mary Jane Chandler. In December 1870 Thomas Waller and William Baxter were charged with 'being quarrelsome and disorderly in the Castle beer-house and refusing to quit when requested by the landlord.' According to the court report, there had been a dispute between the defendants and some foreign seamen and soldiers and women

> who were all dancing, along with the defendants, to music played by a blind fiddler. The defendant said that while they were dancing one of them accidentally stamped on the toes

of one of the foreigners who wanted to fight. They denied refusing to leave the Castle when the landlord George Chandler asked them to, and alleged that Chandler had brought the case against them 'through spite, that Chandler was accustomed to sell rum and gin (he having no spirit license), and as they had threatened to inform against him he had brought this charge.' The defendants were convicted and fined. Chandler went on to become the landlord of the Eclipse. He seems to have had a reputation for drunkenness, appearing in court at regular intervals on various charges of drunkenness and riotous behaviour.

The Castle Inn was put up for sale by auction in November 1875. It was a large establishment – the frontage on Lower Orwell Street was 27 feet, and the advertisement gives a clue to its location 'at the back of the house, with an entrance by folding gates from the Shire Hall Yard and Tooley Street.' It may be that this was the end of the Castle Inn as a public house.

25. Chequer, Westgate Street

A pub of this name was recorded in the parish of St Mary le Tower in the 1689 valuation of Ipswich. It was mentioned in an earlier document of 1574. This is probably the Chequer that stood next to the Griffin on the site of the Crown & Anchor and later became known as the Rampant Horse. In 1726 it was let and described in the advertisement as:

> an Ancient and well accustomed Inn, called the Chequer, Near the Corn-hill in Ipswich with convenient Stables and Outhouses and all other Necessaries, with the Conveniency and Liberty of brewing their own beer, and not being confined to any particular Maltster. Inquire of Mr John Chenery of Needham, Grocer or of Mr Benjamin Freshfield, Carpenter, in St Clement's Parish in Ipswich.

The Chequer changed hands frequently. In 1743, Robert Grimsy bought it by auction and advertised in September of that year,

> The Chequer Inn, in St Matthew's Parish, Ipswich, (a house where any Person for their Conveniency may set up sacks of corn) Is now taken and enter'd upon, where all Gentlemen that will favour me with their Company, shall meet with good Entertainment…

By 1754 it had been taken over by John Conway from the Three White Naggs, Colchester. He appears not to have lasted very long as in 1755 John Woolford, who had lived opposite, was advertising:

> John Woolford, sack and bag maker, is remov'd to the Chequer inn, in St Matthew Street, near the Corn-Hill in Ipswich, Suffolk, which is handsomely fitted up; where all Gentlemen, and others, that will please to favour him with their Custom, may depend on good Accommodation and civil Usage, from their humble Servant, John Woolford. N.B. He carries on the sacking business as usual.

The landlord in 1757 was John Folkard and by 1762–63 Oliver Piggott, who was also a horse breaker and dealer, had taken over. It was still called The Chequer in 1796 when its large yard was used for auctions, but it had been renamed the Rampant Horse by 1802.

26. Cherry Tree, Cox Lane

The Cherry Tree in Cox Lane was a beerhouse that was open between 1735 and 1908.

The Revd Evelyn White made it sound a very attractive drinking place: 'with 38 cherry trees and 400 gooseberry and currant bushes.' In the eighteenth century this part of town was full of gardens and orchards, and this is presumably where its name comes from. It is possible that it went out of use during this time. One advertisement for 'a Messuage or Tenement and Stable, lately an Inn, called or known by the Name or Sign of the Cherry Tree,' in the *Ipswich Journal* in 1758, suggests as much.

John and Lucy Whyard kept the inn from before 1861 until at least 1874. In 1881, the beerhouse keeper was a sixty-year-old widow called Sarah Warren. By the 1891 census, it was recorded as the Cherry Tree Inn and was being run by Henry and Clara Farthing. In 1901, a bootmaker named Harry Catchpole was recorded as living at the same address. Although his twenty-one-year-old granddaughter, Florence Andrews, was described as a barmaid, there's no other evidence to suggest it was still a public house. However, Florence Andrews was described as the landlady of the Cherry Tree in a court case in June 1900. It closed in 1908.

27. Coach & Horses, Upper Brook Street

An inn since the early eighteenth century, the Coach & Horses was a coaching inn and post house with a booking office at the back. According to Leonard Thompson,

> from here such famous coaches as the *Quicksilver*, the *Retaliator*, the *Shannon*, and the Norwich Day Coach made their daily departures. For many years the booking was done by George Frost, better known, perhaps, for his paintings of old Ipswich buildings.

A magnificent sixteenth-century building with a gallery, ornate staircase and courtyard, it was believed to have been the mansion of Charles Brandon, 1st Duke of Suffolk. However Thompson states categorically that this building was in fact directly opposite,

This carved wooden date may relate to the origins of the Coach & Horses as a merchant's house. It was not an inn until 1787.

'on the site now occupied by Messrs. E. L. Hunt's establishment.'

An early landlord was Samuel Debnam in 1729, followed by Thomas Crawley, Thomas Alderson and in 1800, John Pennock. By the 1840s the inn was in the ownership of Cobbold & Son. For a long period, when it established itself as an important hotel in the town, it was run by Charles Godball, who had it from 1853 until he retired in 1880. Next door was a beerhouse, the Coach & Horses Tap, which at this time was run by James and Martha Hill. During Godball's tenancy, a thirteen-year-old boy called Alfred Wasp, who worked for him as an errand boy, was convicted of stealing £5 11s from the hotel till and was sentenced to ten days in prison.

By the time James Game had left the King's Head and taken over, the hotel not only accommodated his large family of six sons, a daughter and his mother, but also seven servants. In 1891, another member of the family, Margaret Game, was the licensee. A widow, she lived there with her four children, a barmaid and one servant. Arthur and Laura Crisp ran it in 1901 by which time he was described as a publican and it appears to have been a much smaller establishment. By 1911, it was again well staffed, with a live-in barmaid, servants and an ostler. The tenant was William Hayward. The Coach & Horses closed in 1977.

28. Cock & Pye, Upper Brook Street

One of Ipswich's oldest hostelries and a thriving pub today, the Cock & Pye was mentioned in 1689 property valuation of the town, although it has been altered beyond recognition over time. There have been many elaborate attempts to explain its name. It is likely to be connected to the venue's long, barbaric tradition of cockfighting, an extremely popular practice in Ipswich until it was outlawed. The 'Pye' may refer to a magpie, a peacock or simply a pie.

This advertisement from the *Ipswich Journal*, 14 December 1765 was placed by Thomas Jackson, who was presumably the landlord at this time:

> COCKING, at the COCK AND PYE, Ipswich, will be fought a Main of Cocks, on the 26th and 27th of December, between the Gentlemen of the Town and the Gentlemen of the County, shewing 31 Cocks on each side, & to fight for Two Guineas a Battle.

Other eighteenth-century advertisements give us further clues to the inn's history:

> This is to inform the publick, that John Stockdall is remov'd from the sign of the Dove, in St Hellen's parish, to the Cock and Pye in St Margaret's parish, Ipswich; where all Gentlemen and others, who would favour him with their Company, shall meet with good Entertainment and a hearty Welcome.
>
> 1743

> This is to give Notice to all Gentlemen, Ladies and others, that John Ellet of the Queen's-Head, Ipswich, has now taken the Cock and Pye, late Stockdel's, now neatly fitted up; where all Gentlemen that will favour him with their Custom will meet with civil Usage.
>
> 1748

In 1756, Christopher Corbe ran a 'convenient Landau' from outside the Cock & Pye to Bury St Edmunds during the spring and summer months and, two years later in 1758, William Kalton of Woodbridge advertised that he had taken the business over, adding as a postscript, 'N.B. There is Back-Way for Carriages out of Cross-Keys Street, and a convenient Lodge for them to stand dry, &c.'

Another advertisement of February 1777 describes what the Cock & Pye was like at this time:

> To be lett, that large and old-accustomed Inn, known by the Sign of the Cock and Pye, Ipswich, the premises consists of 5 parlours; 5 chambers; a very large dining-room; good kitchen and wash-house; a handsome bar and good cellars; 4 good stables and a large coach-house at the old rent of £22 per year.

Like most town-centre taverns, it was not immune to the petty crime that plagued Ipswich's innkeepers. In July 1777, what were described as 'three sharpers' went into the bar and ordered a quartern (quarter of a pint) of brandy, after which they 'found means to amuse the landlady with their conversation whilst they picked her pocket of a purse containing 12 guineas, with which they made off.'

Later landlords were Mr Tovell (1796) and Joseph Harris (1830). Soon afterwards, Edmund Powell and his wife Charlotte took over. Powell seems to have been a well-known local character because the artist Samuel Read drew his portrait. By 1839, Charlotte Powell was running the pub alone. George and Mary Tyrrell were the innkeepers in 1851, when they lived there with their five daughters, two housemaids, a nurse maid and an ostler. They were still there in 1855 but in December of that year Tyrrell advertised that he was leaving: 'To be put off, In consequence of the present Proprietor being about to decline Innkeeping.' The inn at this time, he wrote, had 'a commodious and well-arranged Brewery' attached. He was, in fact, bankrupt and appeared in court at the Shire Hall the following July for insolvency.

By 1857, the Cock & Pye's landlord was Alfred Cudding who had moved to the Bear & Crown by 1861, when the landlord was John Ward, originally from Broxbourne in Hertfordshire. Joseph Harris was landlord in 1865 and was involved in a case of deception when Edward Boulding, a representative of Eyre and Co., wine and spirits merchants of King's Lynn, absconded with money he had taken on his employer's behalf. Harris remained there until at least 1874. The tenants in 1879 were William and Christiana Flood and it was called the Cock & Magpie for a few years. In October 1883, Henry Lambert, aged twenty, a driver in D Battery, 3rd Brigade, Royal Artillery, was charged with 'burglariously entering the Cock & Pye Inn,' and stealing postage stamps, seventy cigars, several boxes of cigarettes, along with spirits, and other valuables. William Flood woke up on the morning of the 15th, having heard shouting and scuffling downstairs, and found 'four policemen with their lanterns, and the prisoner behind the outer bar lying on his stomach.' The whole place had been smashed up, and showered with broken glass, and there was a great deal of blood, presumably the result of the struggle to arrest Lambert, who had entered through a window. The case was sent to the Norwich Assizes where Lambert was found guilty

One of Ipswich's most historic pubs, the Cock & Pye.

The meaning of the Cock & Pye's name is uncertain, but it probably relates to the cockfighting that went on there.

and sentenced to six months' hard labour. In gratitude to the arresting policeman, Walter Osborne, Flood later presented him with a black marble timepiece, surmounted by a bronze sphinx.

Under new management, a new 'Posada' bar was advertised in 1887, 'reserved for the use of Gentlemen only.' In an attempt to move up-market, it seems, the tenants explained that they would be offering

> matured wines direct from the wood. ... The Bodega System will be observed throughout, especially in the matter of Dock Sample Glasses, which contain nearly double the quantity of ordinary Wine Glasses. Although the principle object of the New Department is the sale of Wines, Choice Old Whiskey, Brandy, First Class Burton Ales and London Stout will also be served.

This new management was probably Lott and Frances Betts, who ran the Cock & Pye around that time but had moved to the Admiral's Head by 1891. Charles Powling took over from them. By 1900 Thomas Worboys was living there with his wife, Jane, and daughter, Dorothy. Willis Dale (1911–1922) was followed by Harry Cooper, who ran the pub during the 1930s and appears to have revived the name Posada, which seems to have been used intermittently for some time, sometimes actually replacing the Cock & Pye as the pub's name. During the twentieth century, the Cock & Pye became

The modern interior of the Cock & Pye belies its age.

a popular place for football supporters to gather, as it continues to be. In 2001, the landlord Adrian Caldwell, introduced an imaginative way to help fans watching the World Cup on television there by fixing miniature TV screens on to the beer pumps. According to the *Daily Express*, 'Adrian, 35, ... said: "People used to get really bad neck ache trying to watch the main TV when standing at the bar. But my four screens – measuring four inches by three inches – mean they never miss a shot."'

Adrian Caldwell, a very popular landlord whose nickname was Biglove, has been described as 'the glue that held a community together.' He died, aged only forty-seven, in 2012. He had run the Cock & Pye for seventeen years, turning it into the lively town-centre pub that it remains today.

29. Compasses, St Clement's

An obscure inn, the Compasses was mentioned in the *Ipswich Journal* in May 1801, 'At the sign of the Compasses in the Parish of St. Clement.' The name may be a reference to Masonic traditions or to nautical compasses. A notice in 1810 gives a further clue to its location referring to a sale 'on the Ballast Wharf, near the sign of the Compasses.' In an auction in 1835, John Bromley sold mostly household furniture and livestock ('2 pigs, 3 hens and a cockerel') plus a 3-motion beer engine.

In February 1838, the landlord, Mr Burns, was in the police court on a smuggling charge. He had kept some brandy that had been brought into the country illegally. Burns denied all knowledge of it and his wife gave evidence to say that a Norwegian sea captain had given it to her in lieu of payment for his bed. It was rough brandy, she told the court: 'No Englishman could drink it.' The court believed her story but fined Burns £25.

After this date, the Compasses disappeared from the records and it's likely that it either closed or changed its name.

30. Corn Exchange, Cornhill

Previously the Three Tuns, the Corn Exchange Tavern was a popular drinking place, where no doubt people who came to the market place congregated. An early tenant was Henry Horobin and in the 1850s, the landlord was Charles Pask. With his wife Susan, he presided over a large concern. On census night 1851, they had eleven guests, mostly commercial travellers.

Ipswich Corporation purchased the Corn Exchange Tavern in 1861, in preparation for building the new town hall. The furnishings were auctioned off.

> To be sold by auction, on Thursday, 28 March 1861 … without the least reserve (In consequence of the Premises being purchased by the Corporation), all the useful household furniture and effects at the Corn Exchange Tavern; comprising mahogany and wainscot dining, smoking-room, and Pembroke tables; several dozens of mahogany, elm, and other chairs; chimney glasses, two 8-day dials, ditto clock, fenders, fire-irons, &c; twelve birch and japanned French bedsteads; six feather beds, cotton ditto, mattresses, blankets, and bedding, mahogany chest of drawers, wash stands, toilet sets, dressing tables and glasses; large quantity of kitchen and storing requisites; table cutlery etc.

Trade utensils, also sold, included 'a capital 4-motion beer engine, 5-gallon stone spirit kegs' and pewter mugs.

31. County of Suffolk, St Helen's Street

Often known simply as the County, in the early nineteenth century this was the County Hotel, and, as it was directly opposite the public gallows outside Ipswich Gaol, it must have attracted custom from the hundreds of people who used to gather there to watch executions.

The County of Suffolk.

In 1830, the County was run by William Lambourn, but by 1855 it had been taken over by Henry Kidner. His advertisement in the *Ipswich Journal* in October 1855 suggested he had run into difficulties, as he announced that he was taking

> the earliest opportunity of thanking those Gentlemen who so kindly interested themselves in his behalf, and begs to assure them that nothing shall be wanting on his part to merit their future patronage and support. H. K. also feels indebted to the Public generally, and hopes by strict personal attention, as also supplying every Article of the best quality at the lowest remunerative prices, to be enabled to command continuance of their past favours.

The premises included 'an Assembly Room, well ventilated, capable of accommodating 50 persons, well adapted for a club room,' and 'well-aired beds.'

By 1861, the hotel was back with the Lambourn family again. John and Susan Lambourn were the proprietors. They had the County for some years until at least 1871. William and Eva Whittle took over and kept it until 1881. Wrightson Harrison from Doncaster, an important figure in the local Licensed Victuallers Association, was there in the early 1890s and the County continued to change hands frequently with Walter Canham (early 1900s), Arthur Mills (1911–1922) and Augustus Bye (1930s) taking over successively.

In the late twentieth and early twenty-first centuries, the County has long ceased to be a hotel but has continued to have a succession of landlords. Now part of the Adnams' chain, it has been a music venue and a gastropub.

32. Cricketers, Crown Street

The current Cricketers on Crown Street is a popular Wetherspoon's pub. Built in the mid-1930s, it has a curious design that Tolly Cobbold used for several of its houses, which became known as Tolly Follies. Sometimes described as mock-baronial, they were based on the architecture of Helmingham Hall, the home of the Tollemache family, co-owners of the Tolly Cobbold brewery.

The Cricketers in Crown Street. A fine example of what became known as a 'Tolly Folly.'

For a long time a Tolly Cobbold house, the Cricketer's is currently owned by JD Wetherspoon.

There was another Cricketers Inn nearby, also owned by Tollemache, on the corner of William Street and Navarre Street, immediately behind the present Wetherspoon pub. The earlier Cricketer's was a small, working-class public house. Peter Barr was its landlord for many years, listed in trade directories in 1830 and 1869. In 1851, he was a forty-three-year-old Chelsea Pensioner who was born in Woolwich. In April 1859, Barr, who had served in the Royal Artillery, wrote an unsolicited letter to the Secretary of State for War, signed by sixty 'of the principal Hotel and innkeepers of Ipswich,' complaining about 'the loss and inconvenience to which they were subject in consequence of the present system of billeting soldiers' on them and requesting that an increased allowance might be given them. This was granted the following month.

From around 1900 until at least 1912, the landlord was Charles Whitehouse, followed by Arthur Brundle and E. W. Sawyer. The pub closed in 1936, presumably around the time that the new Cricketers was built. Although the area around Crown Street was massively redeveloped, the building (which became a corner shop) was not demolished until 1963.

33. Criterion, Museum Street
A sixteenth-century building, the Criterion was in hands of the Deaves family, who ran it from before 1851 until around 1893, when it was taken over by Edward Flowers, who was landlord until his death in 1908. It closed a few years later in February 1911.

The building that, for many years, housed the Criterion Inn.

34. Cross, Cornhill

According to the Revd Evelyn White, the Cross

> was a former well known Inn or Tavern on the Cornhill, in the parish of St Mary-at-the-Tower; it probably received its name from the Market Cross: or ... the processions ... when according to ancient custom the usual 'beating of the bounds' took place, and a 'cross' mark, graven upon pillar and post, indicated the several boundaries.

In 1730, the famous Mr Pinchbeck exhibited what was described as 'a masterpiece of art and ingenuity' at the Cross Tavern. This was probably Christopher Pinchbeck, a member of a family of clockmakers and inventors from London, who was exhibiting what he described as an 'Astronomo-Musical Clock' at this time. In 1748, William Gledhill announced that he had moved from the Black Bull in Leadenhall Street, in the City of London, to take over the Cross Tavern. He only lasted a few years because the landlord of the Golden Lion moved a short distance to the Cross in 1751.

David Kindred identifies Waterloo House on the Cornhill as the location of the Cross Tavern. It closed around 1775 when it was replaced by a draper's shop belonging to James Beart. Later, after another demolition it was the site of the Bacon, Cobbold & Tollemache Bank, which eventually was taken over by Lloyds. This was then mostly demolished to make way for Lloyds Avenue. The Cross Tavern must have moved elsewhere after 1775, because it was mentioned in 1887, when the Bailiffs and Corporation of Ipswich held a dinner there. It was still on the Cornhill but its new location has not been identified. This tavern closed in c. 1889.

35. Cross Keys, Carr Street

The Cross Keys was a coaching inn in the seventeenth century, although the building was older, and probably built in the sixteenth. Cromwell's troops were billeted there

Waterloo House, now part of Debenhams, is thought to have been the site of the Cross Tavern.

during the English Civil War, but it seems that the Cross Keys was unscathed by the experience. It had enough importance in the town for Carr Street to have been called Cross Keys Street and it was rebuilt in 1887–88, when the old coaching inn was replaced by a newer building which can still be seen although the premises is currently being used as a British Heart Foundation charity shop.

The Cross Keys had a small brewery attached to it during the eighteenth century. In March 1740, it was:

> To be Lett, and enter'd into immediately, the Cross-Keys Inn, in Cross-Keys-Street, Ipswich, a well accustom'd house with a Brewhouse, Cellars, good Stables, Water, and other suitable Conveniences; where may be bought Coppers, Coolers, and all Utensils for brewing five Combs at a time, ready fixed; with a Stock of Beer, Household Goods, and other Goods of the late Tenant decas'd.

In the year of the Battle of Trafalgar, the owner of the Cross Keys was a Mr Read. By 1820, it was being run by Mr and Mrs Bryant, although Mrs Bryant died that year. In 1838, Charles Lewis Robinson took over the Cross Keys but quickly became involved in controversy when his vote in a parliamentary election was disputed. Ipswich was what was known as Rotten Borough, and many of its elections were extremely hard fought with allegations of corruption flying back and forth. In February 1838, the Whig candidate, Henry Tufnell complained that Robinson's vote in favour of Fitzroy Kelly, the Tory candidate, was not valid. At this time, the right to vote was based on ownership of property and it was alleged that Robinson had not been in full possession of the Cross Keys at the time of the election. It was decided that Robinson's vote was

The upper floor of this charity shop is all that is left of the Cross Keys, an inn and hotel that dated back to before the Commonwealth.

invalid, although it is clear that he was not claiming his ownership of the hotel falsely, because he continued, along with his family, to be at the Cross Keys until at least 1841. William Sadler was the landlord in 1851, but by 1854 he was selling up: 'All the Household Furniture, Feather Beds, Trade Utensils, and Effects of Mr Sadler, at the Cross Keys Inn. The above Old-established Public-house to let, with immediate possession.' He was still the landlord in 1855 however. In the 1860s William and Emma Cooper ran the inn, the premises now occupying numbers Nos 24–28 Carr Street. By 1871, Louis Clayton had taken over.

In 1874, John Freston, who was also a 'horse and gig letter,' was the licensee but he died in late 1876. His widow, Elizabeth continued to run the Cross Keys for many years afterwards. She was still listed as the landlady in a trade directory of 1888. At this time, the old, sixteenth-century, Cross Keys building was knocked down and an application was made in November 1888, by F. A. Cobbold to Ipswich magistrates that 'the license of the Cross Keys might be made final.' The Carr Street Improvement Co. was formed in 1887 specifically to buy up properties there and replace them with shops. Cobbold provided a statement from the architect, Mr Cotman that the building was 'just upon complete' and he was granted the license. However, his bid to be able to open at five o'clock 'there being a good many workmen in the locality,' was rejected. At the end of the nineteenth century, nobody mourned the loss of what was yet another of the town's beautiful old buildings.

Later landlords were Frederick Makin (1890s), Frederick Harris (1900s), Ada Maud Wilkins (1911–12), John Pizzey (from around 1916), Lucy Simpson (early 1920s) and Harold King, who was listed as its proprietor in the 1937 edition of Kelly's Directory at the old address of No. 22 Carr Street. The Cross Keys closed in 1938. It may have been in business for 300 years.

36. Crown & Anchor, Westgate Street

Built on the site of several very old and significant inns, the Griffin, Rampant Horse and the Chequer, this was a hotel for many years under the name of the Crown and Anchor, and is now a branch of WH Smith. It still has a very grand doorway and ornate carved stone lettering from its days as a hotel.

The Griffin was one of Ipswich's oldest inns. It appears in records dating back to 1528 and was mentioned in the 1689 rate valuation when one Nico Walker paid £18 as the Griffin's owner. It was famous for the theatrical performances that were held in its large yard, particularly after 1728 when the landlord, Mr Selby, erected a booth there. The stage collapsed only a year later in 1729, prompting the publication of a pamphlet denouncing theatre-goers. In 1741, the popular 'Rummer wine cellar' opened next to the Griffin. In 1756, landlord Stephen Kirby died and his daughter Ann Trott took over with her husband, Charles.

The Chequer must have been next door to the Griffin and it is also mentioned in the 1689 valuation. It had become the Rampant Horse by 1802 when Thomas Pratt moved from the Bell on the corner of Westgate Street and the Cornhill. Its new name may have been good marketing, as horses, and related goods, were certainly being sold from its premises by 1810. It features in a rhyme about pubs in the Cornhill/Westgate Street area, which obviously appeared after 1802:

> The Rampant Horse shall kick the Bear,
> And make the Griffin fly,
> Turn the Bell upside down
> And drink of the Three Tuns dry.

An early reference to the name Crown & Anchor was in the *Suffolk Chronicle* of March 1811, suggesting it had recently changed hands and been renovated:

> Thomas Duell, Crown & Anchor Inn, (late the Rampant Horse), Begs leave to inform his Friends, and the Public in general, that his House, Stables, &c. having lately been genteely fitted up with considerable improvements, he can now offer every accommodation.

It was sold by auction in July 1815, and at that time had occupied sixty-three feet of frontage on Westgate Street, and contained

> a very handsome coffee room, and two parlours in front; a bar tap room and three other rooms; a spacious kitchen, washhouse, sculleries, store rooms, larder, excellent cellars, and wine vaults, 2 exceedingly good billiard rooms, dining room fronting the street 36ft long, 11 bed chambers, and other dining rooms with attics, a large yard.

It also included extensive stabling and a blacksmith's. The tenant was George Crisp.

During the 1830s, the hotel was run by Thomas and Susannah Harrison. The old building was demolished in 1838 and rebuilt in the 1840s. The ornate neo-Gothic front was not added until much later in around 1897–98. The design of the stonework

Above: Now a branch of WH Smith, there has been an inn on this site since Shakespeare's time.

Right: This ornate door gives away this shop's earlier life as a busy Ipswich hotel.

was probably the work of a local architect, T. W. Cotman, nephew of the Norwich School artist, John Sell Cotman, who was also responsible for the similar work on the nearby Lloyds Chambers and the Cross Keys in Carr Street, among other Ipswich buildings. It was designated as a Grade II-listed building in 1972 and the government's heritage department described the stonework:

> The former hotel has a stone-clad façade. The bottoms of the windows echo the decoration on the Ducal Palace in Venice and the front is decorated with roundels, banners and coats of arms. These are supported by twin lions and display the hotel's emblems, and anchor with crown above. The curved lettering above the doorway is set on the balcony whose jambs are decorated with a vine and grapes.

The hotel was kept by John Oddie Kemp from at least 1871, but by 1891, his wife Rebecca was a widow and running it along with the bookkeeping assistance of her sister-in-law, Emma Kemp, and several domestic servants. Next door was the Crown & Anchor Tap run by William and Charlotte Ellis. After many years in the hands of Birmingham-born Charles Quilter (from approximately 1900 until 1922), the hotel became part of the Trust House chain, later Trust House Forte.

In August 1961, the Crown & Anchor Hotel featured in an important criminal trial in Ipswich, when George Madsen, Niven Craig, and Edward Bonner, all from Essex, were charged with assaulting Francis Mowle with intent to rob him and being equipped for burglary. Detective Constable Willingham said that he and other officers went to the entrance of the Footman & Pretty department store, next to the Crown &

The back of the Crown & Anchor, where long ago a theatrical booth provided entertainment for the people of Ipswich.

Anchor on Westgate Street where, after speaking to a night watchman, they decided to search the premises. They found a briefcase and a wireless set on the roof and at 2.30 a.m., he went to the Crown & Anchor and found one of the defendants hiding behind a service hatch. This must have been William Bonner, as Madsen and Craig were arrested separately. What made the case more notorious was that that Madsen and Craig had been part of a mass escape from Wandsworth Prison in June that year. The ensuing court case revealed that, along with housebreaking equipment, they were carrying gelignite.

37. Curriers Arms, Curriers Lane

The area around the Mount in Ipswich was where leather manufacturing took place and so it is not a surprise to find an inn dedicated to the curriers, who carried out the process of dressing leather after it had been tanned. The origins of this public house are obscure. It was known as the Druid's Head between 1811 and 1816. This unusual name possibly relates to it being a meeting place for the United Ancient Order of Druids, one of many philanthropic societies that were popular in Ipswich. The order was founded in 1781 and Ipswich was the first place outside London to set up a branch.

It was under this name that the inn was offered to let in February 1830. At that time it was apparently bringing in £200 a year. It was quickly snapped up by John Chamberlain, who moved to Ipswich from Washbrook. He was also a farrier and continued working as one while running the Curriers. It was not a success, however. By July the same year, Messrs Toosey, Safford & Co. were advertising the inn again and by November 1814 it was being sold along with a number of other Ipswich public houses.

The Curriers Arms does not seem to have been so lucrative that its landlords could manage without another trade. After John Foreman (1823–1827), the tenants were in succession William Holder, a butcher (from 1830 to around 1855), James Artis (1861), James Smith, a cabinet maker, landlord from 1865, followed by his widow Kelurah, in around 1881. She also kept it as a lodging house, and there were thirty-two guests staying at the Currier's Arms on census night 1881. In 1888 the landlord was Ambrose Harper, also a greengrocer, who was there until after 1892. In 1900 Mrs Sarah Weaver was the landlady, followed by William Kitson (1901) and Ernest Dennis (1904–1916). The last known landlord was George Cant in 1922. The house was owned by Cobbold's for some time until it closed in 1928.

38. Dog & Partridge, St Margaret's Plain

Possibly having begun as a beerhouse called the Partridge, this inn was recorded in 1841 as being the home of George Hunt, a carpenter. In the 1870s, this address was the premises of the Green Dragon public house kept by James Long. It seems to have reverted to its old name a few years later and was known as the Dog & Partridge from 1880 onwards. In February 1880, Ipswich magistrates granted the transfer of its license from William Cotton (deceased) to Barnabas Chilver.

By the late 1880s it appears to have expanded from beerhouse to lodging house and in May 1889, an inquest was held into the death of James Potter Offord, a forty-four-year-old army pensioner, who had been lodging at the Dog & Partridge for more than a month. His body had been found in the Gipping, 'just on the freshwater side of the first lock gates.' Another lodger said that he had seen the deceased on the morning of his death and he had asked him for the money but he had never said anything about wanting to commit suicide. Most of the dead man's clothes were found on the tow path. It appears that Offord did not wish to return to his lodgings because he could not afford the rent and he had been depressed. Another fellow lodger, William Tye, a carpenter, said he had told him that the landlady, Mrs Gray, would always give him a bed even if he didn't have any money but he had refused to return home. The verdict was that he drowned himself while of unsound mind.

A photograph taken in 1900 shows the Dog & Partridge with a group of soldiers and their horses outside. Next door was the premises of a smith, George Cook, who shoed the horses from the nearby barracks. By 1930, it was no longer a public house of any kind, being the shop of Frederick Osborne, boot maker. The houses on both sides were boarded up and scheduled for demolition. It was closed at some time between 1923 and 1930.

39. Dog's Head in the Pot, Upper Brook Street

Dog's Head Street in Ipswich is named after this inn. Its name may have been unique to Ipswich although there was a Dog & Pot in Stoke Poges. One explanation of this name was that it related to the traditional sign for an ironmonger, which depicted andirons and a pot. Andirons were the metal stands that supported burning wood in a fireplace and were commonly known as 'fire-dogs.' Another popular interpretation of the name is that it refers to a slovenly cook allowing a dog to lick the cooking pot, or is from a Dutch proverb about someone who is late for dinner and arrives after the meal has been given to the dog. The first explanation seems most likely, given that many early inn signs related to trades and occupations, and this particular one was on the route to the busy shopping area. In addition, neither of the other explanations – the slovenly cook or the guest losing his dinner to the dog – would to have been attractive to potential customers of a tavern.

An early reference to the Dog's Head in the Pot dates back to 1612 and 'Dog's Head in the Pot Lane' was marked on a town map dated 1674. Descriptions of the inn suggest that it was an odd looking building which had a large and rather fanciful turret on the Brook Street side.

It is unknown when the Dog's Head stopped trading, but it has been suggested that it became the White Hart and Punchbowl which was certainly somewhere nearby. An inn was described by this name in the *Ipswich Journal* in July 1749, when Joseph Mills informed the Ipswich public that he had moved to the Ram Inn on the Common Quay. A new landlord arrived in 1762, when William Truss 'Late Servant to Wm. Berners Esq; has taken the White Hart and Punchbowl in St Stephen's, Ipswich, (lately occupied by Mr Edward Bennett) being a commodious House and neatly fitted up.' Edward Bennett had gone to the Saracen's Head in Bury St Edmunds. In July 1770, it was described as 'an antient and well-accustom'd Publick House.' It was sold four years later, advertised as 'A Freehold Messuage, formerly known by the Name of the White Hart and Punchbowl, situate near the Blue-Coat-Boy … with a Tenement adjoining, now in the Occupation of James Pilkington.'

Nothing remains of the Dog's Head in the Pot inn except the street that was named after it.

For many years the Ipswich Building Society had its premises on the site. Strangely, the modern buildings that replaced the long disappeared Dog's Head have been given an equally curious and inexplicable turret.

40. Dolphin, Quayside

Mentioned as early as 1528, when it was known as the 'Dolfin,' in a document about the payment of rent for its sign, the Dolphin closed in 1909. The name has been used for other drinking places in Ipswich, including inns in Duke Street and Lower Orwell Street, but it appears to have been a fixture in the dock area.

In 1874 it was advertised to let: 'The Dolphin Beer-house, situate on the Quay, Ipswich. Large Yard and Stables, where a profitable Carting Business has been carried on for more than 30 years.' Old photographs show it nestled up against Paul's massive maltings. In 1910, already closed, the Dolphin was badly damaged by a fire that had started in Paul's.

41. Dove, St Helen's Street

Currently a very popular pub trading under the name of the Dove Street Inn, its interior is much older than the outside, which dates back to at least to the early eighteenth century. It was advertised as

> a Good and well accustomed Inn, known by the Name of the Dove in St Hellen's Parish, Ipswich, the Stock of Beer and Brewing Utensils, with the Household Goods to be Sold as they shall be Appris'd by two indifferent Persons. Inquire at the said House, or at the White Elme at Copdock, Suffolk.

John Stockdall was the landlord until 1743 when he went to the Cock & Pye. By 1750, William Coe had taken over but was selling the Dove again, as did John Wood, nine years later, with a 'Bakehouse adjoining.'

For many years, between around 1830 and 1851, Obadiah Lucas, from Harwich, held the license, followed by John Thurlow (1855), Emma Thomas (1861) and then the Bird family who ran the inn from around 1865 until 1874. In 1872 the landlord, Alfred Bird, was fined £2 1s when he

> was charged with allowing intoxicating liquors on his premises after ten o'clock on the night of Sunday, 25th. A policeman visited the defendant's house at the hour mentioned and asked if all was going on right. The defendant replied that it was, but the policeman found some half-pint mugs with some beer in them and five men were seen to leave the house by the back way.

Pembroke Larter was innkeeper here from about 1879 until 1904. Described in one census as a pensioner at the age of forty-four, he was probably a former soldier. By 1911, the landlord was Horace Mayhew, who was succeeded by his son, Stanley, who grew up in the Dove, and kept it until the early 1930s.

For most of the twentieth century the Dove was in the hands of the Young family, George Young in the 1930s, and Leonard Young in the 1950s. For a while, during the 1990s, it was known as the Tap & Spile, under the tenancy of John Wiseman, but it has since returned to its old name, or at least the similar Dove Street Inn, and has been transformed into an award-winning and very popular Ipswich pub. A brewery was opened there in July 2011. In recent years it has also become a venue for meetings of the Ipswich Town Supporters Club.

The ever-popular Dove Street Inn.

A room built on to the back of the Dove belies the building's probably seventeenth-century origins.

An unusually empty bar at the Dove.

42. Drum & Monkey, Princes Street

A modern public house, which mainly caters to sports fans – it is close to Ipswich Town FC's stadium – the Drum & Monkey was previously known as the Sporting Farmer. Before becoming a car park, the land at the back of this building was the site of the New Cattle Market so the name was presumably designed to attract both the farmers who attended the market and the sports fans who came to Portman Road.

According to CAMRA historians, its first license in 1961 was transferred from the Three Swans, which was at No. 83 Princes Street, possibly close to where Riley's pool hall is now. The idea that it had previously been known as the Four Swans appears to have come from a census enumerator's mistake.

In June 1870, two ten-year-old boys, Charles Bloomfield and Charles Hill, narrowly escaped three months' imprisonment when the landlord, Isaac Norman, of the Three Swans brought a case against them of throwing stones that had broken his windows. The land in this part of Ipswich was still largely marshes, and Norman did a great deal himself to try to improve the roadway around his pub. The Three Swans was run for many years, from around 1879 until 1939, by the Boughton family.

43. Duke of Kent, Upper Orwell Street

The Duke of Kent began in what looked like an ordinary house in the early nineteenth century, but when it was rebuilt in 1903 it had something of an early 'Tolly Folly' design about it. It is likely that it was named after Queen Victoria's father, the Duke of Kent and Strathearn.

The tenant was William Skeet in 1830 and, although William Skinner was listed as the landlord in the 1855 White's trade directory, William Skeet was still landlord in 1865 and

A modern pub close to Ipswich Town's football ground, the Drum & Monkey succeeded the Sporting Farmer and the Three Swans around this part of Princes Street.

kept the house until at least 1874. In December 1866, James Smith, a stonemason was found guilty of beating Skeet with a poker. The defendant denied the charge but claimed that he argued with the landlord because he allowed other customers to sing. From 1879, the Duke of Kent was run by William Orford Penny, who was still there in 1901 at the age of seventy-nine. The address in 1901 was still No. 6 Upper Orwell Street, so presumably the change to No. 10 was made after demolition, as part of the Major's Corner redevelopment, and rebuilding around this time. After it was rebuilt it was sometimes described as a hotel and many of its guests were visiting seamen who were waiting for their ships in the port.

From around 1937 until the late 1950s, the landlord was Walter Hare and it has been described as a lively pub that was 'always full of customers.' The Duke of Kent was closed by Tolly Cobbold in November 1965.

44. Eclipse, Orwell Place

The Eclipse was on the corner of Orwell Place and Upper Orwell Street. Famously, Orwell Place had a pub on each corner and was close to the Unicorn Brewery in Foundation Street. It may have been named after a famous racehorse which won several major races at Newmarket in the late eighteenth century. Alternatively, it may have been named after HMS *Eclipse*, a 169-ton gunboat that was launched in 1797. In 1861 William and Lucy Sugars were running the premises as a beer shop, after which the Eclipse was run for many years by Henry Cornelius Burgess and his wife, Elizabeth. They were there in 1871 and were in business until May 1888. Henry, then aged seventy-three, died from a chill, which he caught at Ipswich Races according to the local newspaper. In his will, Henry left his entire estate of £45 12s 6d to his son, James, who took over the Eclipse.

The Duke of Kent, now a community centre.

By 1891, James and Ellen Burgess were running what was described as a beerhouse. It was a small street corner pub with one bar. In 1901, Ellen Burgess, now widowed, was the publican, assisted by her daughter Florence and sons Arthur and Ernest. They were still there in 1911.

The Eclipse closed on 13 January 1923.

The Eclipse was once here, as were three other Ipswich pubs, one of each corner of this busy junction.

Between life as the palace of a local dignitary and bishops and the present row of shops, this was the site of an inn called the Elephant & Castle.

45. Elephant & Castle, St Nicholas Street

The Elephant and Castle stood on the site of Curson's Palace, which stood on the corner of St Nicholas Street and Silent Street, the home of the extremely wealthy and powerful, Sir Robert Curson. After Curson's death in 1535 it was used as the Bishop of Norwich's palace. It was a naval hospital named the King's Hospital in the 1660s, during the Dutch Wars. The first mention of its use as an inn is in a parish perambulation in 1750, which recorded a malting office behind the old palace porch with land known as the 'Elephant Orchard.' In the late eighteenth century, Robert Trotman, a maltster, was shown as the tenant. He bought the property from the diocese of Norwich in 1799 for £263 10s. It was gone by 1809 when a sale of timber there referred to 'Premises formerly the Elephant and Castle.' Little is known about this inn, apart from a reference by Thomas Martin in *c.* 1740 to Curson's arms being carved 'upon the low sell (a carved bressummer beam) of a window at the [Elephant and] Castle Inn in Ipswich.' Today, it is hard to imagine that this was such a historic site as there is no trace of it.

46. Falcon, Falcon Street

An early reference to the Falcon can be found in the *Ipswich Journal* of August 1728:

> This is to give Notice that on Friday the 16th Instant, there will be a Gun of Five and Twenty Shillings Value, shot for at the Sign of the Falcon, in St Nicholas Parish in Ipswich, by any Gentleman, or others, with a single Ball, standing a 100 Yards, and to shoot with such Pieces as they shall bring themselves.

John Curtis moved to the Falcon from the Cock & Pye in 1743 but it seems to have changed hands a year later when James Osborn took over from Curtis who had died. The Bowman family ran the Falcon from before 1816, probably until Alfred Bowman's death in July 1857. In *Eighty Ipswich Portraits* (1980), historian John Blatchly wrote of Robert Bowman Jnr:

> Like his father, the third Robert was brewer, wine and spirits importer and coal merchant of the Falcon Inn and the Brewery on the corner of Queen Street and Falcon Street. The inn is there today, although totally rebuilt. Both father and son were Liberal councillors in their turn.

During their time at the Falcon, the inn appears to have been involved in all kinds of electoral machinations related to the Bowman's Whig sympathies. The elder Robert Bowman sat on many important Ipswich committees. In 1816, he took out an advertisement in the *Suffolk Chronicle* thanking the public for supporting his breweries, presumably with an eye on his electoral ambitions:

> Falcon Brewery, Ipswich. Robert Bowman returns his best thanks to a generous Public for the favours so liberally conferred upon him since the establishment of his Brewery, and announces his intention of *dropping the price of his Beer*, immediately upon the additional Malt Duty being taken off.

After the Bowmans, the Falcon Brewery was owned by Bridges, Cuthbert and Company and the inn had a succession of tenants. J. Cracknell ran the Falcon until Charles Bradley took over in August 1869. He was landlord until the late 1870s when William Gardiner and his Liverpudlian wife, Elizabeth, became tenants. Thomas Orris

Bowman's, originally called the Falcon, on the corner of Falcon Street.

ran the Falcon for a short time between 1881 and 1883 before handing the license over to Henry Austin Barham, who kept the pub for many years. He was still there in 1922. Walter Fooks was landlord from the 1930s until the 1950s.

The inn remained the Falcon until 2004 when various new names were tried. It has been known as Tonic and Bar Pl@tinum. In choosing Bowman's, the current name, after a revamp in 2010, the current owners have, at least, given a nod towards the inn's history.

47. Fox, Upper Brook Street

Unrecognisable today – it is a bookmaker's – the Fox Inn was a substantial building which may have dated back to the seventeenth century. In the 1850s, it was run by Henry and Lucy Haken. After Henry's death, Lucy took out the following notice in the local newspaper in December 1859:

> Mrs Haken, while returning thanks to her Friends and the Public for the Favours, so many years enjoyed by herself and late Husband begs to recommend Aaron Martin, from Carlisle, well known that City, for their support.

By March 1861, Martin had gone and James and Jessie King were keeping the Fox. At this time it was a substantial enough business for them to be able to employ a live-in barmaid, house servant and pot boy. In 1891, the Fox was run by Emma Codd and her sister Elizabeth Abbott.

The last owner of the Fox was Tolly Cobbold and it closed in 1970.

The sign of the Fox Inn (courtesy of the Brewery Tap).

48. Galliot Hoy, Fore Street

On the junction of Fore Street and Lower Orwell Street, the intriguing name is a combination of two types of vessel that served the Port of Ipswich. Galliots were Dutch one-decked schooner type ships, many of which frequently came to Ipswich, and hoys were small vessels that serviced the galliots, taking goods and passengers out to them. Leonard Thompson described the inn as having 'lofty rooms, and characteristically Tudor high-pitched gable and three dormer windows. Its life as an inn is believed to have dated from early in the 17th century.' In 1843 the pub changed its name to the Prince of Wales. Photographs do not remotely resemble Thompson's description, so it had been substantially altered by then. When the building was demolished in 1893, it became the premises of Sneezum's pawnshop.

49. Globe, St George's Street

A seventeenth-century listed building, currently owned by the Ipswich Building Preservation Trust, who restored it after it had stood empty and neglected for many years. It was for several centuries known as the Globe Inn, although in the early eighteenth century it had been known as the Hat & Feather. The road was known for many years as Globe Lane. Between 1811 and the late 1840s, it was called the Bricklayer's Arms and owned by William Blasby, who, despite being a shoemaker, owned several properties around the Crown Street area.

In 1865 Mrs Harsent, the landlady of the Globe, was sued by customer Samuel Smith, who had left his coat and bag there. Mrs Harsent said that she had given the

This old postcard shows Fore Street, a street of many public houses, including the Neptune.

The Globe Inn, which had been the Hat and Feather, is now a hairdressing salon.

coat to a policeman, but the coat was never recovered. Smith claimed £1 compensation, alleging that the coat was lost by negligence. The case was dismissed.

For much of the twentieth century, the Globe was in the hands of the Quinton family. David Quinton was licensee from 1911 until around 1932 when Arthur Quinton took over. It was a Tolly Cobbold house and closed in 1958.

50. Golden Fleece, St Matthew's Street

Along with cockfighting, the cruel sport of bull baiting was popular in Ipswich. It took place on the Cornhill and at the Golden Fleece, also known as the Fleece, until it was banned in 1805. The Fleece was a large building. It advertised that it had stabling for sixty horses in the 1840s.

For many years, Elijah Mead was innkeeper. He was landlord in 1830. He also kept a coaching business, which he sold to William Webster in 1865. Mead was still there in 1874. The Towns family ran the Golden Fleece for many years from 1879, Mrs Ada Towns from at least 1888 until around 1912, although sometimes the licensee is named as Arthur Towns, her son. He continued the business until the mid-1930s when Thomas Barden took over.

It closed in September 1962 and was bought from Tolly Cobbold via a compulsory purchase order by the Ipswich Corporation who then had the building demolished.

51. Golden Lion, Cornhill

A very old inn, next to the Town Hall, the Golden Lion was originally called the White Lion. A tax document of 1571 refers to the 'Whit Lion at ye West Ende of ye Mote

Hall' owned by John Sherman. Only eight years later it was called the Golden Lion in town records: 'The signe of the Golden Lion shall continue paying yerely to the Towne 1d rent.' In borough accounts, also of the Elizabethan period, it was included in a list of items in the custody of the town's Treasurer 'in the west house under the halle next the Lyon.'

In August 1769, it was advertised for sale: 'To be Sold The Golden Lyon Tavern, situated on the Corn-hill in Ipswich. For further particulars enquire of Mr Cha. Norris, in Ipswich aforesaid.' In 1846 John Garrod took over, as the tenant of Mr Fox. The hotel was a substantial affair employing eight servants, including an 'underboots.' Its proximity to the Corn Exchange must have brought invaluable business. Fox put the Golden Lion up for sale in 1870, Garrod having been there for twenty-four years. The auction, run by Fox & Garrod, was attended by a large crowd: 'The bidding commenced at £2,000, and after spirited competition, the property was knocked down to Mr John Garrod, the present landlord, for £3,710.' Garrod died in September 1880.

The hotel eventually went into the ownership of Tollemache and was for many years a thriving commercial hotel. It had extensive stabling at the back that can still be seen although it has long since ceased to be used as such. Part of it was used as a nightclub called the Betty Ford Clinic in the 1990s. The Golden Lion extended to abut Mannings, but since it was sold to Wetherspoons, part of it has been used as a noodle bar. In July 2015, Wetherspoons announced that it was putting the Golden Lion up for sale.

An unusual angle of the Golden Lion building, now housing a Wetherspoon's pub, a hotel and a noodle bar.

Originally called the White Lion, the Golden Lion is one of the oldest hotels in Ipswich.

52. Great White Horse, Tavern Street

A great deal has been written about the Great White Horse already, mainly because Charles Dickens wrote about it in *The Pickwick Papers*. The White Horse has a much longer history, however, and was the last inn in the 'street of taverns' to close. In medieval times it was known simply as 'the Tavern.' In 1344, the notorious Roger Bande killed Geoffrey Costyn, a yeoman, after drinking there. They quarrelled on their way back to their lodgings in Holy Trinity Priory (now Christchurch Park).

The White Horse dates back to 1518. In the reign of Elizabeth I, the town accounts recorded that its owner 'paid to Newman the pavor the 28 of Maye for paving against the conditt ageinst Conowaye's dore and ageinst the White Horse.'

In the eighteenth century, it was a coaching inn and in August 1764 the proprietor, Charles Harris, advertised that the Ipswich Post-Coach left for London from outside at 5.00 p.m. every day. The cost was 3p a mile. When Tavern Street was widened in the early nineteenth century, the old, half-timbered building was either demolished or extensively remodelled and faced with white stone. In 1830 the landlord was Henry Guiver, who also rather enterprisingly ran refreshment rooms at the railway station and provided carriages for funerals. If that doesn't sound Dickensian enough, it was around this time that meetings of a curious group of young men called the Rum Pups were held at the White Horse. If they didn't like a speaker, or he went on for too long, members would throw themselves on to the ground and moan loudly while lying on the floor, propped up on their knees and elbows. At first calling themselves the 'Rump Ups,' they adopted the later name when they evolved into a (slightly) more respectable musical society.

Charles Dickens, who didn't like Ipswich very much, certainly didn't enjoy his stay at the Great White Horse Hotel, if his description of it in *The Pickwick Papers* is anything to go by. He began by describing the large statue of a white horse that is still above the front door:

> ... a stone statue of some rampacious animal with flowing main and tail, distantly resembling an insane cart-horse, which is elevated above the principal door. The Great White Horse is famous in the neighbourhood, in the same degree as a prize ox, or county paper-chronicled turnip, or unwieldy pig – for its enormous size. Never were such labyrinths of uncarpeted passages, such clusters of mouldy, ill-lighted rooms, such huge numbers of small dens for eating or sleeping in, but beneath any one roof as are collected together between the four walls of the Great White Horse at Ipswich.

Nevertheless, it was Dickens who made the Great White Horse world famous. So much so, that a full scale replica of it was built at the Chicago World's Fair in 1893 to serve as the British Building. Judging on engravings that appeared in the press at the time, the replica was either of the old building, which had already disappeared behind the white stone renovations, or extremely fanciful. According to Leonard Thompson in his book, *Old Inns of Suffolk*, the 'rampacious' statue was removed to the White Horse in Tattingstone and replaced by the version that can be seen today.

The Great White Horse was the headquarters of supporters of the Conservatives in elections. Their Whig rivals met at the Crown & Anchor in Westgate Street. The proprietor, William Brooks, was a leading Liberal who stood for the town council, successfully, in 1839 and 1842. He appeared in a Tory broadside that mocked the local political opposition, which describes the Blues' rivals as animals in a menagerie: 'A singular animal always found near *Brooks*, supposed when first seen to be a *White Horse* but on nearer view was found to be a Great Bear: answers to the name of Silly Billy.'

During the twentieth century, after a long period as a 'county, family and commercial hotel and motor garage,' run by John Harrison, it was bought by Trust Houses Ltd (later Trust House Forte) in 1922. After various attempts to modernise it, this world-famous hotel finally closed in 2008 and has recently reopened as a branch of the American coffee shop chain, Starbucks.

53. Green Man, Key Street
Next door to the Ram, the Green Man was in the heart of the docks. In December 1778,

> a press-gang entered the house of Mr Edward Wiles, called the Green Man ... in order to impress some seamen there, when a scuffle ensued and Mr Wiles was beat in a violent manner, the noise occasioned by the above circumstance brought in Mr Thomas Nichols, the landlord of the Ram Inn on the Common Quay, who expostulated with the gang for their inhumane treatment of the said Wiles, but without effect; The outrage still continued and the said Thomas Nichols received a violent blow on the head with a bludgeon from one of the gang, of which he languished till the next morning about 9 o'clock and then

The Great White Horse, made famous by Charles Dickens, is now a branch of the American coffee chain, Starbucks.

Having been a coaching inn for centuries, the twentieth century saw this entrance converted for the use of motor vehicles.

The Victorian owners of the Great White Horse capitalised on the Dickens' connection with this 'Pickwick' bedroom.

The Great White Horse at the end of the nineteenth century.

died. On Wednesday the coroner's inquest sat on his body, and it appearing the gang have no warrant or other legal authority to impress, and there being no positive evidence of the person who gave the blow, the jury brought in their verdict of wilful murder against the gang who are all committed to our gaol to take the trials.

Another murder, in 1843, made the pages of *The Times*, after the body of Hayward Ling, a travelling brush salesman, was found floating in the dock. Thomas Coles, landlord of the Green Man gave evidence in court that Ling had been drinking there but had left with Charles Cole, a stranger, intending to go to the Dove. Moments later, they heard a cry and a splash. It was alleged that Cole pushed Ling into the water in an attempt to rob him. Cole was convicted of manslaughter and transported for life.

The Green Man closed in 1911.

54. Greyhound, Upper Brook Street and Henley Road

The original Greyhound, or Le Greyhound as it was then, is said to have been the oldest inn in Ipswich. Revd Evelyn White claims that it was probably rented from one of Ipswich's priories. It was almost opposite the Buttermarket, near to the Cock & Pye, and was mentioned in documents of the early fourteenth century. It appeared frequently in the town accounts in the late sixteenth century, because its owner William Lymefeld was an important figure in the town. He was Chamberlain of Ipswich in 1573–74. Business was often done at his tavern, such as: 'Paid to William Lymefeld the 19 of Auguste for wyne geven by Mr. Bayliffes to all the justices' in 1571–72.

A short description of the inn appears in *Ipswich 200 Years Ago*, a transcript of an assessment of Ipswich made for tax purposes in 1689:

> It appears that this tavern had a considerable frontage in the street and a large garden and premises behind, and there is every reason to conclude that all the premises in the entrance to them next to the Coach and Horses formed part of 'Le Greyhound' property.

The assessment also recorded that £50 was paid by Gilbert Lingfield, for the Greyhound which was owned by Jo Rycroft. This valuation was the same as that for the manor, park and gardens of Christ Church, which indicates how valuable a property it was.

Knightly Wood ran a wine-cellar there in 1729 and it is thought to have been open until at least 1845, but nineteenth-century references to the Greyhound or Hound give the address as St Margaret's Green. There may also have been a Greyhound beerhouse on the Quay at this time.

The present Greyhound on Henley Road also appears to have had several locations, although it may be that it was the streets that changed rather than the inn. In the Victorian era, the area around Anglesea Road and Fonnereau Road was extensively developed, changing it from what was a predominantly rural area, and a major route out of town, to a significant residential area, that included the nearby barracks and East Suffolk Hospital. Directory entries that list the Greyhound as being in Nos 9–11 Salem Street or St George's Street, also known as Globe Lane, probably refer to the current building or a predecessor.

In 1830, the landlord of the Greyhound, was John Airey, originally from Debenham, who was a tenant of John Morphey. The Greyhound, 'with Tenement attached' was sold by auction in 1842 presumably with Airey as sitting tenant. He was still landlord in 1861, although the 'Greyhound, Anglesea Road' was listed in 1855 as being run by W. Lankester. In 1861 records, the address was Henley Road. Airey was living there with his wife, Frances and five children.

The award-winning Greyhound in 2015.

The bar staff of the Greyhound in the 1950s (courtesy of Richard Mainwaring & Dan Lightfoot).

The lounge bar of the Greyhound on Henley Road.

William Cotton, who was landlord in the 1890s, had a sideline hiring out horses and carriages of various kinds: 'brakes suitable for cricket and other parties, bean fests; … broughams, landaus, Victorias and open carriages on shortest notice.' In the early twentieth century, the landlord was William Castleton, who took over from Scotsman, James Nicholson in 1911–12. Castleton kept the Greyhound until at least the outbreak of the Second World War. The second half of the twentieth century saw it become the haunt of doctors and nurses from the nearby East Suffolk Hospital, either drinking inside or using the off-sales door which was where the front bar is now. Mr Ken Lightfoot, a regular for many years, told me that doctors who were on call would sit in the Greyhound and go straight back to theatre when needed. The problem of hygiene was at least mitigated by the fact that the landlord in the 1950s had served on a destroyer, the HMS *Alamein*, and the floorboards were cleaned to naval standards.

Sylvia Capon, a twenty-one-year-old nurse made the front page of the *Daily Express* in 1953 when she popped into what was described as the Greyhound's 'off-licence department.' For this, she was summarily dismissed from her job: 'Mr. T W Bland, Chairman of the Ipswich Group Hospital Management Committee, said: "Miss Capon's engagement was terminated because of a breach of a well-known unwritten rule."'

Suffolk brewers, Adnams bought the Greyhound in 1980 and, in 1988, it was altered considerably when part of the building was turned into a private dwelling. For many years there was a red telephone box outside the door to the front bar but it was removed around ten years ago. Since the Greyhound was taken over by Dan and Emma Lightfoot in 2011, it has become an extremely popular, award-winning pub, famous for its hospitality as well as the high quality of its food and drink.

55. Grinning Rat, St Helen's Street

Previously the Olive Leaf, this pub dates back to the seventeenth century, although the building was substantially altered in the nineteenth century. The original name, which may be unique to Ipswich, probably relates to the Dove Inn and Dove Street, both close by, and the Biblical story of the Dove returning to Noah's Ark with an olive leaf as a symbol of peace.

Its first recorded landlord, when it was a beerhouse, was Walter Dade, who kept the Olive Leaf from at least 1830 until after 1861. This was a very poor part of Ipswich during the Victorian era with most residents recorded as labourers, even paupers, in the census returns. Thomas Skerritt, a Yorkshireman, was landlord in the 1880s.

More recently, the Olive Leaf became a thriving gay venue, although the controversial eviction of landlord James Iannone by Punch Taverns in 2013 led to him moving to the Arboretum.

56. Gun, Upper Brook Street

This inn existed in the seventeenth century, somewhere between Le Greyhound and the Cock & Pye, but very little else is known about it.

There was another Gun Inn at No. 19 Key Street, equally as old, and mentioned in the 1689 assessment as the Gunn, owned by the Widow Harrison and in the possession

Above: The Grinning Rat, formerly the Olive Leaf.

Right: The Grinning Rat's modern sign.

of John Jours. This very old building was demolished in 1875 when the *Ipswich Journal* informed its readers that

> a much-needed and desirable improvement, and one that will be agreeable surprise, is surely to be made in Key Street, Ipswich. The old public house known asked the Gun, which has filled the angle of the two streets, Key Street and Lower Orwell Street, from time almost beyond memory, is being pulled down, and a handsome edifice, pointed with stonemasonry, of which Messrs. Gibbons and Messrs. Chinnock have the design, and Mr Cotman is the architect, is to take its place. The owner of the property is Mr J C Cobbold, of Holy Wells, and he is now rebuilding it. The old house is in a very dilapidated state, and has been so for some time past.

It added that the Gun had been an 'eyesore for some time.' The Gun Inn eventually became the Gun Café and closed in 1940.

57. Half Moon, Foundation Street

Standing on the corner of Foundation Street and Lower Brook Street, the Half Moon was a fifteenth-century merchant's house converted to an inn. It may have belonged to Henry Tooley, whose considerable wealth was used to build almshouses and help the poor. It was a thriving public house for several centuries, but closed in 1913. The building was demolished soon afterwards despite huge protests. All that remains is a carved corner post depicting a fox preaching to geese which is in the possession of Ipswich Museum. Oak panelling and a superb carved mantelpiece were also saved and taken to the Cobbold family home at Holywells.

58. Half Moon & Star, St Matthew's Street

Supposedly dating back to the seventeenth century, the Half Moon & Star was a substantial building. Its proximity to the local barracks meant that it was a popular choice for soldiers.

The Half Moon and Star, an old coaching inn and hotel, now converted to flats by the Ipswich Buildings Preservation Trust.

In its early days it brewed its own beer, but that seems to have been over by 1736, when it was advertised for rental, along with two houses 'fit for Private Families, and … a Smith's Shop, with a pretty Dwelling,' all for £18 a year. In the late eighteenth century, it was a venue for cockfighting. The landlord John Blumfeild offered a prize of a pair of silver buckles for the winner of a fight there in December 1748. In 1798, it was possible to see a dentist called Mr Crawcour there, who advertised that 'His Dentifrice Tincture and Powder may be had of him' at the inn for the remaining few days of his visit to Ipswich.

In the 1850s there was a granary at the back and its yard and stables were used for horse trading and the hiring of cabs, often leading to allegations of wrongdoing which ended up in the local courts. George Fenn, who was licensee here between 1888 and 1901, was principally a farmer. His son Thomas took over what was then the Half Moon & Stars Hotel until the 1920s.

The hotel closed in 1985, after which it was purchased by the Ipswich Buildings Preservation Trust who, in what they described as their 'largest project to date,' converted it into four flats and a cottage with money from the Heritage Lottery Fund.

59. Hermit, King Street.

This was a beerhouse on the corner of King Street and Elm Street. The address was sometimes given as No. 1 Elm Street. King Street in the nineteenth century had several inns, including the Swan, the King's Head and the King's Head Tap. The Hermit closed in 1921 and the building is now a café opposite the Arcade Street Tavern.

60. Holly Tavern, Cooks Row

The Holly Tavern was one of several medieval taverns and wine shops owned by the Malyn family. It stood in Cook's Row which is now Dial Lane and Chaucer's grandfather, William Malyn, inherited it. Ipswich historian Vincent Redstone tells us that

On the corner of Elm Street and King Street, the Hermit was next to the even older Swan.

William Malyn is mentioned in the will of Alice, relict of Philip Harneys, as William de Dennington, proprietor of the Holletavern (Holly Tavern) standing in Cook's Row, Ipswich. After the death of Isabella Malyn, her son, Robert le Chaucer, of London, held the tavern...

In March 1338, when Albreda Malyn, widow of William, kept the Holly Tavern, a Mr Roger Bande came into the tavern to discuss a dispute about other property 'and with a stroke of his sword almost amputated her right hand.' Albreda died of her wounds, but Bande escaped punishment.

Chaucer's grandparents also owned a wine shop opposite the Holly Tavern, where H&M now stands on the corner of Tower Street.

61. Insolvent
One of dozens of town centre beerhouses, virtually nothing is known about the Insolvent, but it seems worth recording for its ironic name alone. It was open in 1735.

62. Isaac's, Wherry Quay
Isaac's, a large pub in a converted malting, was once owned by merchant Isaac Lord. It stands on the quayside, and has an enclosed courtyard and bars on two levels. Formerly the Malt Kiln & Cobbolds on the Quay, the building dates back to at least the late eighteenth century. It has become very popular, particularly since the improvement of the docks area and the arrival of students at University Campus Suffolk.

The Holly Tavern was somewhere at the corner of Tavern Street and Dial lane, formerly Cook's Row. This was also the site of an inn called the Mitre.

Popular with students, Isaac's was named after the Ipswich merchant, Isaac Lord.

63. King's Arms, Thoroughfare

Sometimes confused with another King's Arms on the Cornhill, this inn, run by Henry Lee between 1830 and 1855, was 'pulled down for extensive alterations' in 1872, although the *Eastern Counties Chronology* of 1906 states that it was demolished completely in 1879. Kindred says that it was previously the Three Coneys and, before that, the Eight Bells, so it appears that the name change may have occurred after the demise of the Cornhill inn. At the top of the thoroughfare, it was the last public house in Ipswich to refuse to serve women. It was closed by Tolly Cobbold in August 1966 and has been turned into shops. The upper floor is a Hindu Temple.

64. King's Head, King Street

The King's Head was sited at the same spot as where the Corn Exchange now stands. An inn of the same name was on this site from at least 1528, when records show that its owner paid rent for having its sign on the street. In 1689 it was assessed at a value of £35 and 'in the wid. Coles occupacion.'

The famous coach, 'the Original Blue' left from here and it was another inn that held cockfights in its yard. The nineteenth-century building was not old, although it was substantial. Next door was an older pub called the Sickle and the King's Head Tap was presumably on the other side. They were all demolished in 1880 to make way for the Corn Exchange.

65. Leopard, Crown Street

A typical Victorian street pub which had beautifully engraved glass windows advertising whisky and brandy and a huge lamp above the door, it was located at Tower Ditches or Tower Terrace. There was a Leopard in Crown Street in 1757. Run by Mary Ann Trew and Thomas Trew from 1839 to 1871, Mary Ann continued alone after Thomas's death. It closed in about 1923.

The slightly unusual name is generally thought to be a reference to the trade of weaving, although the weaver's arms have three leopards. Interestingly, the heraldic crest of Thomas Wolsey also had leopards' heads.

66. Lord Chancellor, Greyfriars Road

Another town centre inn with a nominative connection to Ipswich-born Thomas Wolsey, who was Lord Chancellor of England 1515–1529, this rather ordinary public house received some notoriety in 1896 when its landlord, James Butcher gave evidence at a trial for attempted murder. The defendant, John Chittock, had stabbed his estranged wife, Matilda, because he couldn't afford maintenance payments. Butcher told the court that Chittock, had walked into the bar and 'holding out his hand said "I come to shake hands, and to wish you goodbye; I've done it." Witness said "Done what?" To which he replied "Murdered my wife."' He received eighteen months hard labour.

The Lord Chancellor closed in December 1914.

67. Lord Nelson, Fore Street

Only three of St Clement's inns and beerhouses have survived out of fifty-two that flourished in the nineteenth century. The Lord Nelson is one of them. Called the Noah's Ark in the eighteenth century, it changed its name when Admiral Nelson was appointed High Steward of Ipswich in 1801. The building dates from the seventeenth century, though a new brick frontage was added later following flooding. Although there have been substantial alterations over the years, it still retains many of its original features and has a charming courtyard at the back which is next to St Clement's churchyard.

In 1890, following the death of the brewer Owen Ridley, it was advertised for let at £14 a year. Eventually, it was acquired by Tollemache and was a Tolly Cobbold pub for many years until Adnams bought it in 1989.

68. Manning's, Cornhill

Manning's is a narrow building dating back to the sixteenth century. It lies between the Golden Lion and the large Victorian building that was the Bell. The bar, which was knocked from two rooms to a single long bar in 1981, runs a long way back to a small garden at the rear of the pub. Upstairs there are still remains of original Jacobean panelling.

At various times, it has been known as the Victoria or Manning's Victoria. John Spooner Manning was a wine and spirits merchant recorded at the premises from 1830 to 1855. He was born in Ipswich in 1784 and retired at the age of seventy-one or seventy-two. He died in January 1858, leaving everything – £3,000 – to his son, James Manning, who was a manufacturing chemist in Newton-by-Willows, Lancashire. He was succeeded at Mannings by Mary Ann Nicholson, and then by various members of the Nicholson family.

In more recent times, Manning's has been a popular meeting place for football fans, including the members of the Scandinavian supporters' clubs who travel to Ipswich for matches.

Above: The Lord Nelson.

Right: Local hero – the Noah's Ark was renamed to celebrate the Ipswich connections of Admiral Nelson.

Above: Manning's unusual and attractive wrought-iron sign.

Left: A perennial Ipswich meeting place, Manning's.

Below: The bar at Manning's.

69. Marquis of Cornwall, Old Foundry Road

Also known as the Marquis Cornwallis, and named after Charles Cornwallis (1786–1793), a British army officer who was, among other things, the Lord-Lieutenant of Ireland. There is a local connection. He commanded the East Suffolk Regiment of Militia, based at Ipswich, during the 1820s.

Among its tenants were John and Hannah Stevens (1823–1844), James and Mary Ann Last (1851), Folkard and Sarah Pendle (1871), Henry Fisk (1879–1891), Robert Williams (1900–1904) as Henry and Emily Lloyd (to 1916).

It was a very attractive street corner pub with a rounded end, which closed in 1954 and is now a corner shop.

70. Mulberry Tree, Woodbridge Road

The current building dates back to 1928, although there was a Mulberry Tree on the site since at least 1830. A rare pub name, there being only one other, in north London, it changed its name to the Milestone in 2002, but reverted to its old name in 2012. For many years it has been a popular venue for local bands.

Among its landlords were John Oxborrow (1830), John Stearn (to 1860), Mary Ann Hartridge (1855), George Addison (1900–1916) and the Jarman family from 1928 until around 1937.

71. Neptune, Fore Street

The beautiful Neptune building dates back to the fifteenth century, but has been altered since. The date 1639, painted on the front, probably refers to rebuilding, although it could be the date it changed from a merchant's house to an inn. Writing of the Neptune in 1888, Dr J. E. Taylor said:

The Mulberry Tree which was renamed the Milestone for a while.

Perhaps the most notable part is the present tap-room. The quay labourers sit over their beer in a carved-ceiled, oak-panelled room, the mantelpiece of which is good enough to lead to the sin of covetousness. Upstairs, the Front room has a plastered ceiling, modelled in sections, with the Tudor Rose as the chief ornament. The back of the inn is evidently of older date than the front.

Sailor's wages were paid in the Neptune bar in the eighteenth and nineteenth centuries, when they presumably spent most of their earnings in the pub. It had a reputation for being involved in smuggling, which may be merely romantic, but given the frequency and violence of smuggling in Ipswich at this time, it is not unlikely. Some of its tenants were: Walter Podd (who died in 1789), James Hurwood (1830), Nicholas Wellen (1855) and George Green (1900). Its last landlady was Matilda Jarrett, who ran the Neptune from about 1932 until it closed in 1937.

72. Old Bell, Stoke Street

Despite having long been an eyesore, the Old Bell was one of Ipswich's oldest and most historic inns. It may have been called the Sea-horse. A carving of a sea-horse by 'eminent Ipswich wood carver, Mr. Ringham' was found there and restored. Revd Evelyn White claims that it was on the site of a bell foundry. Before Stoke Bridge was built, the Old Bell was only accessible by a ford through the river.

The Old Bell was in existence in 1639. A town assembly book for that year contains this entry: 'The posts lately erected by John Cole, Ship Carpinter, in the Streete before his house in Peters Parish, against the Bell shall stand at the rent of 6d.'

This postcard view of the Neptune shows what it was like when it was still a tavern.

The Old Bell is currently closed but has a long history as a dockside public house.

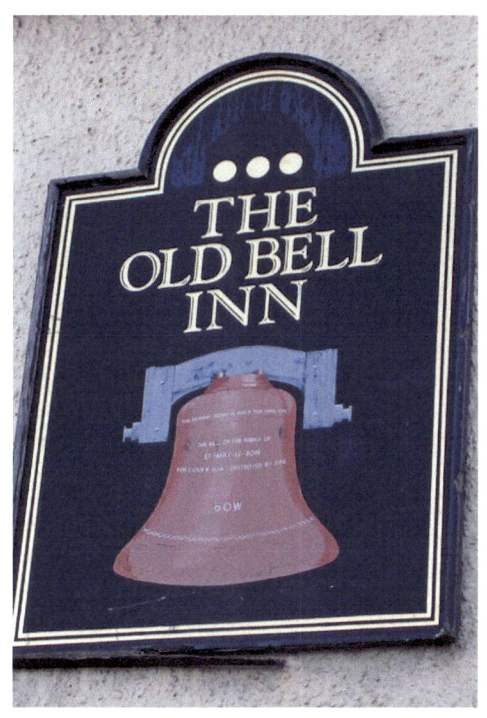

It is thought that the Old Bell was on the sight of a medieval bell foundry.

The sign of the Old Bell.

In the nineteenth century, it was another cockfighting venue with a clientele that was notorious for violence. In the 1870s, the landlord, Edward Baldry, told a court that he was terrified of one notorious customer who would frequently smash the inn up after drinking there.

When the Old Bell closed in 2007, it had been the oldest inn in Ipswich, an honour that then passed to the Spread Eagle in Fore Street.

73. Oxborrow's, St Peter's Street

Another timber-framed seventeenth-century building, it was the home of Sir Manuel Sorrel, a Portman and Bailiff of Ipswich in the 1660s. Oxborrow's was previously called the Plough & Sail, the name is a link between the two commercial aspects of Ipswich. Edmund Oxborrow kept the Plough & Sail in the 1870s and 1880s, but the name-change took place in the 1930s when Capt. Henry Horne took over and turned it into a hotel. It closed in the 1980s, although a failed attempt was made to run it as St Peter's Restaurant. It is now the offices of Seven Asset.

74. Pack Horse, St Margaret's Plain

The Pack Horse Inn stands just outside what is Christchurch Park, and dates back to when it was the location of an Augustinian Priory, Holy Trinity, which flourished until Henry VIII seized the Priory's estates in 1536. Travellers to the Priory would stay at the Pack Horse. It remained an inn throughout the centuries, long after the Dissolution of the Monasteries and the building of Christchurch Mansion. In 1936, a substantial portion of the building was demolished and the remainder was turned at a right angle to allow for road widening. It is now an estate agent's offices.

A place of rest for pilgrims and visitors to Ipswich's priories, the Pack Horse is now an estate agent's.

75. Paddy McGintys, Northgate Street

Until it became an Irish pub in 1988, McGintys was known as the Halberd, a name that is still proclaimed in large green letters on the outside of the building. The current building dates back to the seventeenth century, although the roughcast facings on the outside are nineteenth. It is still possible to see parts of the town ramparts and the North Gate in the back walls. Its name is unique to Ipswich. A halberd was a Tudor weapon, a combination of an axe and a pikestaff.

76. Plough, Dog's Head Street

By the Old Cattle Market, now a bus station, the Plough is another old Ipswich tavern, dating back to the seventeenth century. Among its later landlords were John Barber (1830) and Isaac Norman (1855). In 1900, Frederick Farrow took over as landlord. He had been the manager of the Ipswich Reform Club for many years. After suffering from influenza in December 1899, he appears to have become mentally ill, suffering from what were described at the inquest as great anxiety and delusions. In a tragic turn of events, Farrow drowned himself in the Gipping leaving behind a moving letter telling his family what his intentions were.

The Plough changed its name to Blades during the 1980s. When it reverted to the Plough, it adopted a short-lived policy of refusing to sell lager. Since 2000, it has been owned by Pubmaster.

77. Portobello, Lower Orwell Street

Like the Admiral's Head, this pub's name has a connection with local hero and MP, Admiral Vernon. The Porto Bello was his ship. The inn once had a painted sign that

Paddy McGinty's, an Irish pub, which was for many centuries known as the Halberd.

The bar of Paddy McGinty's.

Rear view of McGinty's clearly showing remains of the old North Gate.

The Plough in Dog's Head Street.

Above: The interior of the Plough has recently been refurbished.

Right: The Plough's sign portrays Suffolk's agriculture and Ipswich's engineering history.

depicted the ship and was sold in 1754 as a 'freehold messuage, some time since known by the sign of the Porto-Bello … with a small Piece of pasture Land adjoining.' According to police evidence to the Brewster Sessions in 1896, it was close to the Plough and only sixty-seven paces from the Spread Eagle. It was mentioned in a court case of 1843, when Henry Garrod and John Curtis, from Bucklesham, were charged with causing a disturbance after they tried to take a horse into the bar.

78. Post Chaise, Woodbridge Road

The Post Chaise was at the corner of Woodbridge Road and St Margaret's Street. Its name presumably related to its use as a coaching inn and its situation on a main route out of town.

In March 1888, the landlord, Arthur Ayres, was convicted of assaulting William Girling of Tuddenham in the inn. The judge added in his closing remarks that he was considering referring Ayres to the public prosecutor for perjury.

The Post Chaise was closed in 1926 and for a while was a furniture store. After that closed, it remained in a sorry state of dereliction for some time until it was demolished in 1933. It was on this site that the nine-screen Odeon cinema was built.

79. Rainbow, St Matthews Street

On the corner of St Matthew's Street and St George's Street, this was a large street corner public house, dating from the late 1850s, when it was known as the Rainbow Inn. It was always a place where soldiers from Ipswich Barracks drank. During the

Second World War, black US serviceman used the bar as the American authorities insisted on segregating their troops. White soldiers used the Queen's Head.

In December 1960, what *The Times* described as 'six Jamaicans' were tried at the Central Criminal Court in London for the murder of the Rainbow's barman, Maurice Britton, who was stabbed during a fight there. Wesley Smith and Henry Atkinson were found guilty of manslaughter and sentenced to eighteen months' imprisonment. Later Smith appealed on the grounds that he was outside the pub at the time of the killing, throwing bricks in. The Rainbow never recovered from this incident and it closed permanently in November 1961.

80. Ram Inn, Quay Street

The Ram 'is an ancient and curious house,' wrote the Revd White, 'There is a tradition ... that the grewt [sic] and benevolent Henry Tooley was born there.' A previous occupier of the Ram was one Noah Bloomfield, a Bell-founder, who advertised his incoming by stating that he had fitted up the house 'in a genteel manner but intended to carry on the Bell Foundry as usual.'

In 1822, newspapers reported that a two-year-old child had been snatched from its mother in Harwich and the abductor had jumped onto a ship bound for Ipswich: 'He might be heard of at the Ram public house which is kept by Smith.' Shortly after that, Thomas Cuckow, who was also a sail-maker, was landlord, followed by William Bellhorn in 1855. In 1891, Jane Orford was recorded in the census as the innkeeper there. She may have been the last. Another sixteenth-century pub, the Ram closed in around 1892.

81. Rep, Tower Street

The Rep, also known as the Old Rep, was originally built as a lecture theatre for the Ipswich Mechanics' Institute in 1879. It has a wonderful construction inside, with ornate galleries and Charles Dickens gave readings there several times. In 1909, it became Poole's Picture Palace but when that failed in 1947 because of the considerable competition from Ipswich's many other cinemas, it was converted into a theatre. A repertory company, Ipswich Arts Theatre, was based there for many years until it moved to its permanent home in the purpose-built Wolsey Theatre in 1979. Among the many stellar theatre careers that began here were those of Sir Ian McKellen, Sir Trevor Nunn and Pam Ferris.

It was reopened as a pub in the 1990s and was refurbished by new owners Greene King in 2013.

82. Rose, St Peter's Street

The Rose was another very old Ipswich inn, mentioned in the 1689 tax valuation. In 1730 it was described as 'a very commodious House, With good stables, Real office and utensils, ready furnished together with a large seller and a good stock of beer.' When its landlord Martin Carrington died in 1805, he was in some debt. Robert Spalding and his family ran it until sometime before 1861. In 1883, the landlord Thomas Blumfield was found to be drunk and disorderly outside his own pub. He told the court that he:

The Rep has recently been taken over by Greene King.

The lovely interior of the Rep, still reminiscent of its past as a lecture hall and theatre.

Another view of inside the Rep.

The Rep's sign hints at its past as Ipswich Arts Theatre.

did not deny having had a little to drink. He had a few words with his wife in consequence, he said, and she went out, taking the keys with her. He went to Ganter's [neighbours], for the purpose of getting the keys. He would have been alright if the constables had left him alone.

He was fined 20s.
At the end of the nineteenth century the Ipswich Working Men's Mutual Independent Federation and the Ipswich Harriers held annual dinners there. It changed its name to the Rose Commercial Hotel and hired out cabs. Part of what is a very beautiful building was demolished in 1903 when St Peter's Street was widened. The remainder is now a Grade II listed building. It closed in 1969 and is now offices, next door to another pub, the Thomas Wolsey.

83. Royal Oak, Northgate Street

This magnificent building became the Royal Oak when its license was transferred from an inn of the same name in Tavern Street in 1689. The landlord for many years was William Flory, who in 1861 placed a notice in *Ipswich Journal* giving his

> sincere thanks to the Nobility, Clergy, Gentry, and to the public in general for the kind patronage and support accorded to him during the last Eighteen Years, and begs to assure them that nothing shall be wanting on his part to merit a continuance of the same.

Flory also supplied coaches, gigs, Phaetons, dog carts and cabs from the premises.

Another of Ipswich's oldest inns, the Rose.

The Royal Oak closed in 1882 by Cobbold & Co., and the building was bought by local architect, T. W. Cotman who restored the building considerably.

84. Running Buck, St Margarets Plain

Mentioned in a 1689 valuation as the Buck, it was also known as the Roe Buck, and eventually became the Running Buck. There was a brewery on the site because, in 1853, the landlord William Jannings, sold the brewing equipment at auction, because he was 'quitting.' It was kept by the Ashford family from around 1855 until at least 1881.

In 1887, a new landlord, William Hobbins, held a house-warming to celebrate taking the inn over. Among the toasts given were: 'Success to the Running Buck Harmonic Meetings.' The newspaper report of the party described an 'especially pleasing incident during the evening's proceedings was the performance of Miss Lepronia A. Baker upon the handbells.' Music was also performed there from the 1960s to the 1980s when a nightclub called Canes operated from a log cabin built at the back. The whole enterprise closed in 1991 and the building is now a community centre run by the Besthesda Baptist Chapel.

85. St Jude's Tavern, St Matthew's Street

Opened in 2011, in connection with the St Jude's brewery, which has since closed, this award-winning establishment is probably more like a Victorian beerhouse than a traditional pub. It was previously a photographer's studio.

86. Salutation, Carr Street

One of the oldest inn names in Ipswich, going back to the time of Ipswich's shrine, the present Salutation goes back to the eighteenth century. In March 1733, it was offered for sale as:

The Oak, no longer an inn, but still a remarkable building.

Very little has changed from this early twentieth-century postcard view, except the motor car.

This carved wooden corner post is a good example of an art form that used to be found all over Ipswich.

Above: The Running Buck is now run as a meeting place by the Ipswich Betgesda Chapel.

Right: St Jude's Brewery Tavern.

a very good Messuage, with a handsome large Garden, late in the occupation of Mrs Tye, deceas'd; a Tenement adjoining with an extraordinary good Malting-Office and all Conveniences; a very good accustom'd Inn, call'd the Salutation, all in good repair and well tenanted.

John Rolfe announced that he was leaving the Salutation to become landlord of a pub in Woodbridge in October 1769. In June 1828, George Gooch of the Salutation, advertised that he was selling off his 'horses, gigs and effects' by auction to pay his debts. In September 1847, 'Sarah Susannah Crickmere was charged with having stolen seven blankets, the property of Mr Simon Sharman, landlord of the Salutation Inn, Ipswich. The prisoner was a native of Lowestoft. She had lodged at the Salutation, and, upon her leaving, the blankets were missed, and afterwards found pledged at the house of Mr Frazer' (a pawn shop). The following year, an inquest was held into the death of

> James Farthing, aged 56, a butcher in the employ of Mr Andrews, Buttermarket. On Thursday, the deceased, who lodged at the Salutation Inn, was seized with pains in the back, stomach and chest, which continued until early yesterday morning when he vomited a great quantity of blood, and gradually expired ... brought on by habits of intemperance.

It appears that the landlord John Stannard may have lost his license in 1861 after committing perjury when giving evidence in a trial the previous year. A much more

There has been an inn called the Salutation in Ipswich going back to the time of its medieval Shrine to Our Lady of Grace.

The depiction of Thomas Wolsey on the Salutation's sign is misleading. It is more likely to have been named as a reference to Ipswich's shrine to the Virgin Mary.

recent and happier event took place in 2015, when Bob Williams celebrated being the landlord of the Salutation for forty years.

87. Saracen's Head, St Margaret's Green
Standing by St Margaret's church, the Saracen's Head was mentioned in the 1689 valuation, but its name suggests earlier origins. Victorian photographs show the large public space outside crammed with wagons and, in 1756, a steelyard was erected there to weigh goods that would then be sold and carried out of town. The same year the keeper of the town gaol, Jones Erdington, became landlord. Other tenants were Robert Bedwell (1840s), William Russell (1850s) and Robert Keeble (1860s). The Harrison family ran it from about 1874 until 1892. After Thomas Garwood was landlord in the first years of the twentieth century, the Overton family took over until the mid-1930s when William Youngman became tenant. This very old inn closed in October 1960 and is now a business centre.

88. Ship Launch Inn, Ship Launch Street
There may have been two pubs of this name, one in Key Street and then other on the corner of Cliff Road and Ship Launch Road. It was a purpose-built public house, catering for the workers in the docks and the St Clement's area. An early landlord, from between 1830 and 1855, was William Curtis. It is no longer a public house, but a Chinese restaurant called the Golden Ship.

89. Spread Eagle, Fore Street
Since the closure of the Old Bell, this is the oldest inn in Ipswich. It probably dates from the sixteenth century. In 1747 it was sold 'with a good Slaughter-House, good Conveniences for Brewing and all Brewing Utensils.'

Among its tenants were Abraham Wolsey, who ran it from 1840. After his death, his widow Matilda continued until at least 1855. It appears to have had a butchery

Saracen House, formerly the Saracen's Head.

The Ship Launch gave its name to the street, but it is now a Chinese restaurant.

connection for many years. Several landlords, including George Copping (1865), Frederick Field (1869–1881) and Arthur Keeble (1900–1911) were also butchers.

It was refurbished in 2015 and remains a lively town centre pub.

90. Station Hotel, Burrell Road

Despite its promising location, opposite Ipswich Railway Station and backing onto the river Gipping, this public house and hotel has not always been successful. In recent times, it has been home to an Indian restaurant, and it has had several changes of name. It was the Riverside from 2011 until 2015.

It opened in the Victorian era, and its landlady in the 1860s was Maria Fisk, who ran it as a 'family and commercial hotel and Posting house.' She employed a housemaid, an ostler and a cook. Carriages would stand outside to pick up passengers who arrived in the town by train. At the end of the nineteenth century, players at Ipswich Town Football Club would change at the Station Hotel, as facilities were extremely poor at Portman Road. A group of Victorian footballers jogging across the bridge to Princes Street and the football ground must have been a sight to behold.

91. Sun Inn, St Stephens Lane

Even now, it's possible to see what a lovely location the Sun – sometimes known as the Rising Sun – was. First documented as an inn in 1458, it was a private home before that. The present building, is probably a little later, perhaps sixteenth century. Situated between St Stephen's Church and the Cattle Market, many of its customers were drovers and cattle dealers.

Among its landlords were: James Biddell, who moved from the Tankard in 1749; James Gull, who took over upon the death of Philip Stephens in 1855; William Burrows in the 1860s and 1870s; and Mary Mullett, who was landlady in 1900.

The Spread Eagle is Ipswich's oldest public house following the closure of the Old Bell.

The Station Hotel.

Closed by Cobbold's in about 1917, it became an antiques shop and then a bookshop named Atfield and Daughter. A glimpse into its courtyard shows the beautiful pargetted Sun sign that is still on one of its walls.

92. Swan, King Street

Leonard Thompson wrote:

> It existed when the borough's total number of inns was only 24. It was originally timber-built with a heavy overhang at the first floor, and with its richly carved timber work and leaded windows it was undoubtedly a picturesque building. The front is known to have been altered several times during the past three hundred years, and the date, 1707, to be seen superimposed on the plasterwork, probably refers to the last of these alterations.

The lovely old courtyard of the Sun Inn with its pargetted sign.

The Swan is still eligible to pay a fine of 40s (£2) to the trustees of a charity called Parker's Gift for a murder that took place at the inn in 1664. The original penalty was intended to provide coals and assistance to the town's poor. In 1999, when the document was discovered in the archives of St Mary-le-Tower, the tenants agreed to continue to pay the fine, saying 'We like being part of history.'

93. Tankard, Tacket Street
Opened in 1736, and also known as the Theatre Tavern, it was rebuilt in 1802, but finally demolished in 1961. Before it was a tavern, it was the family home of the aristocratic Wingfield family and very richly decorated as a result. As with many of the houses his company owned, John Cobbold took much of its valuable and interesting interior away to his own home at Holywells.

It is most famous for its connection with the Tankard theatre and the fact that it was here that actor David Garrick made his stage debut.

94. Thomas Wolsey, St Peter's Street
A beautiful seventeenth-century building, with a large courtyard at the back, the Thomas Wolsey is close to where the Cardinal was born. It has had several different names including the Craftsman, the Toad and Raspberry and Raps. In the early 1990s, it was owned by former Ipswich Town and Scotland footballer, Alan Brazil and called the Black Adder, after the popular TV comedy series.

95. Three Feathers, Westgate Street
In the Middle Ages, Ipswich had a shrine dedicated to the Virgin Mary, known as Our Lady of Grace, and almost as important as the one at Walsingham in Norfolk. Thousands of pilgrims flocked to Ipswich and many taverns sprung up to cater for them. The shrine was destroyed in the Reformation and there is no trace of it now, except for a neglected narrow alleyway called Lady Lane.

The Swan is much older than the date of 1707 that can be seen on the wall.

One of the Tankard's grand rooms taken from Clarke's History of Ipswich.

One of many pubs named after the Ipswich-born cardinal, the Thomas Wolsey is thought to be near to his birthplace.

Above: The Thomas Wolsey's side entrance through which coaches and carts would enter.

Left: The courtyard behind the Thomas Wolsey.

On the corner of Lady Lane is a 1970s brick building, currently a 'pound shop.' This is where the Three Feathers stood. The inn can be traced back to 1528. On either side of the street were taverns, the Three Feathers on the south side and the Three Kings, on what now is the corner of St Matthew's Street. Both inns obviously were in a prime position to attract the custom of pilgrims and other visitors to the town. Between them was the West gate, which, until 1794, was a large stone construction – big enough to hold the town gaol – through which visitors to Ipswich from the west passed.

The original building was demolished in about 1780, but there was a public house on the site until 1966. It went under various names: The Three Feathers, the Prince of Wales, the Prince of Wales Feathers and the Feathers. In 1740, the Three Feathers was mentioned in an advertisement, which referred to the landlord, Thomas Bolton. In January 1758, a carpenter published a notice in the *Ipswich Journal* alleging that

> Richard Chapman, of this Town, Inn-holder, did, on the 7th Day of December last past, in the House commonly called the Three Feathers in Ipswich aforesaid, with a great oaken Plant, beat, wound and ill-treat, Daniel Driver of the same Place, House Carpenter; and upon his endeavouring to defend himself from the violent Blows that he received from the said Chapman, that he the said Daniel Driver had one of his Fingers broke in a terrible manner in two Places, and used in such a cruel Manner by the said Richard Chapman insomuch that he goes in Danger of his Life; and whereas the said Richard Chapman did on the same day abscond from the said Town, and has been seen up and down at Claydon, near Ipswich aforesaid. He is a blackish man, about 5 Foot 10 Inches high, and born at Kennitt, near Bury St Edmunds in the county of Suffolk; he was dressed in a brown Duffel Coat over a blue-grey Coat, Buckle-Leather Breeches, and a dark brown Wig. Whoever apprehends the said Chapman so that he may be brought to Ipswich to Justice, shall receive an Reward of Two Guineas, to be paid by William Driver of Ipswich aforesaid, House Carpenter.

It is not known whether Chapman was brought back from Claydon, but the aggrieved Mr Driver was still placing the same appeal in the newspaper two months later.

The Feathers was in an ideal place to serve the coach and carriers' trade. In 1796, John Clarke begged 'leave to inform his Customers that his VAN will set out from the Three Feathers inn, St Matthew's, Ipswich, every afternoon to Colchester.' A wagon left from here on which goods and parcels could be sent to London. It operated twice a week in 1838, and guaranteed a twenty-four-hour delivery.

In the nineteenth century this was a working man's club and the venue of meetings of various friendly societies and trade union gatherings, such as the annual 'Rivetters' Soirée' for the National Union of Operative Boot and Shoe Rivetters. Their 1877 meeting was a particular success, and the landlord, William Price, was praised for 'a most substantial repast, served in excellent style.' Price was landlord for many years, from about 1880 until 1916.

Towards the end of its days, there was a slaughterhouse at the back, and it closed, along with a number of other Tolly Cobbold houses in October 1966.

Francis Grose's eighteenth-century illustration shows the Three Feathers (right) and the Three Kings on either side of the West Gate.

96. Woolpack, Tuddenham Road

The Woolpack, then at Bolton Lane, was mentioned in 1689 valuation. Something of a country inn, it was a popular with people travelling into town as it was cheaper for them to stable their horses there, rather than pay at the nearby toll house. Built in the middle of the sixteenth century it stood alone, according to Leonard Thompson, 'the nearest house to it would have been Hervey's farm, which stood on the site now occupied by Hervey Street. [Nearby] ... stood a long wool warehouse. Later this warehouse was converted into stables by the ... Fonnereau family.'

When the toll house disappeared, the Woolpack converted its extensive stables to a slaughterhouse. Originally a wooden building, the new inn was among the first brick buildings in Ipswich. There were several accidents outside the Woolpack in the nineteenth century. Henry Rose, an ex-soldier, was killed following drunken horseplay; when he fell out of the door and down the stone steps, hitting his head. The landlord, William Turner, was lucky to get away with a verdict of misadventure. At the end of December 1868, a thirty-five-year-old horseman, Charles Taylor was killed just outside the Woolpack when he fell off his wagon. Although witnesses declared him 'completely sober,' Taylor had drunk two pints of mild with his breakfast at the Saracen's Head.

In March 1855, an advertisement stated: 'To be let, the Woolpack inn, with immediate effect, in consequence of the death of the landlord.' Applicants were invited to contact Cobbold & Son, of Brook Street. The new landlord, John Dowsing, announced he was 'putting off' the Woolpack and moving to Liverpool. He appealed to those who owed him money to contact him to settle up. In March 1871, George Turner auctioned off the fittings and effects belonging to the tenant, Mr Mullinger, as the incoming landlord didn't want them.

After several years of neglect, the Woolpack has been rejuvenated and is now a popular place to eat and drink, close to the gates of Christchurch Park.

The Woolpack.

Above: Inside the Woolpack.

Left: The sign of the Woolpack.

Bibliography

Books
Blatchly, John. *Eighty Ipswich portraits.* (1980)
Clarke, G.R. *The history and description of the town and borough of Ipswich.* (1830)
Dunkling, Leslie & Wright, Gordon. *Pub names of Britain.* (1994)
Grace, Frank. *Rags and bones.* (2005)
Kindred, David. *Ipswich: lost inns, taverns and public houses.* (2012)
Thompson, Leonard P. *Old inns of Suffolk.* (1946)

Journals
Proceedings of the Suffolk Institute of Archeology & History, 1869–present
Ipswich Journal, 1720–1902
Suffolk Chronicle, 1810–1871

Web
suffolkcamra.co.uk

Also Available from Amberley Publishing

Explore Ipswich's secret history through a fascinating selection of stories, facts and photographs.

Paperback
96 pages
978-1-4456-4494-3

Available now from all good bookshops or to order direct
please call 01453-847-800
www.amberley-books.com